BANFF
TRAVEL GUIDE

*"This guidebook serves as your essential passport to exploring the Canadian Rockies, featuring comprehensive insights into **Banff and Lake Louise, Canmore, Jasper, and Yoho National Park.** Enriched with vivid photographs, detailed maps, interactive QR codes, and carefully planned itineraries, it provides everything you need to navigate and enjoy these majestic landscapes."*

HARRISON WALSHAW
June 2024 2nd Edition

Copyright © 2024 Harrison Walshaw. All rights reserved.

Copyright Notice: No part of this publication may be reproduced, distributed, or transmitted in any form or by any means, including photocopying, recording, or other electronic or mechanical methods, without the prior written permission of the publisher, except in the case of brief quotations embodied in critical reviews and certain other noncommercial uses permitted by copyright law.

Disclaimer: This Banff Travel Guide is provided for general informational purposes only. Although every effort is made to ensure the accuracy and reliability of the information, the publisher does not guarantee the completeness, accuracy, or reliability of the guide. All content is provided "as is," and reliance on the information in this guide is strictly at your own risk. The publisher will not be liable for any losses or damages arising from the use of this guide, including, but not limited to, indirect or consequential loss or damage, or any loss or damage whatsoever resulting from loss of data or profits arising out of, or in connection with, the use of this guide. Information in this guide may change, and it is recommended to confirm details with official sources and local authorities before making travel arrangements. This guide is designed to assist you in discovering the breathtaking landscapes, vibrant cultures, and unique experiences of Banff.

Embark on your journey through Banff, filled with majestic mountains, pristine lakes, and the warm hospitality that defines the spirit of this renowned mountain paradise. Enjoy your travels across Banff, exploring its rich heritage, diverse ecosystems, and the unforgettable adventures that await.

How to Use This Guide

Welcome to your comprehensive guidebook, "Banff Travel Guide: Embark on an Unforgettable Exploration Discovering the Wonders of Canmore, Lake Louise, Jasper, and the Canadian Rockies." This guide is designed to assist travelers in navigating and experiencing the rich landscapes and diverse activities available in the Canadian Rockies. Here's a breakdown on how to use this guidebook to enhance your travel experience:

Navigating the Guide

Attractions & Detailed Entries: Each location such as Banff, Lake Louise, Jasper, Canmore, and Yoho National Park is detailed with sub-sections that include major attractions, lesser-known sites, and practical visitor information. For each attraction, you'll find historical context, visiting tips, and directions to help you plan your visit efficiently.

Itinerary Suggestions: Tailored itineraries such as "Banff in a Day" or "One Week in the Rockies" are designed to help you maximize your visit depending on the duration of your stay. These itineraries combine various attractions in logical sequences to ensure you experience the best each area has to offer without feeling rushed.

General Information: Sections like "Getting There and Around" provide logistical details to help you plan your journey to and within the Canadian Rockies. You'll find information on transportation options, entry requirements, and more.

Practical Tips: This section offers advice on how to deal with local weather, wildlife encounters, and other safety tips to ensure a safe and enjoyable trip.

Section by Section Use

Banff, Lake Louise, Jasper, Canmore, and Yoho: Each section starts with an overview of the area followed by detailed entries on top attractions. Use these sections to understand the geography, cultural significance, and recreational opportunities available.

Accommodations and Dining: Whether you're looking for luxury lodges or cozy campgrounds, each section provides recommendations and reviews to help you make the best choices for your stay.

Outdoor Activities: Detailed guides on hiking trails, ski resorts, and other outdoor activities are included. This section is particularly useful for adventure seekers looking to explore the vast natural landscapes.

Cultural Insights: Learn about local history, art, and cultural attractions. This includes museums, galleries, and historical sites, as well as insights into local festivals and events.

Practical and Safety Information: Essential reading to understand the dynamics of visiting a natural park area, including how to dress for the weather, navigate the terrain, and respect wildlife.

Instructions for Using the Interactive QR Code Map

Experience the Canadian Rockies with ease! Follow these simple steps to find your way to any attraction:

1. **Scan the QR Code**: Find the QR code and use your smartphone camera or QR code scanner app to scan it.

2. **Tap the Link**: Once scanned, a notification will appear. Tap on it to open/search the location details.

3. **Select 'Directions'**: On the opened web page, tap the **'Directions'** button to get real-time navigation to the attraction.

4. **Start Your Journey**: The map will display the best route from your current location to the attraction, helping you get there without any hassle.

Contents

How to Use This Guide i
BANFF NATIONAL PARK 1
Attractions within Banff National Park 2
    Bow Falls and Bow Falls Viewpoint 2
    Bow Falls to Hoodoos Trail 2
    Cave and Basin National Historic Site 3
    Lake Louise Ski Resort & Summer Gondola 4
    Mount Norquay 5
    Parker Ridge 6
    Sentinel Pass 8
    Sulphur Mountain Cosmic Ray Station National Historic Site 10
    Sundance Canyon 11
    Surprise Corner Viewpoint 11
    The Fenlands Banff Recreation Centre 12
    Lake Louise Sport & Recreation 13
Attractions within the Town of Banff 13
    Banff Park Museum National Historic Site 13
    Buffalo Nations Museum 14
    Historic Luxton Home Museum 14
    Whyte Museum of the Canadian Rockies 15
    Art Of Man Gallery 15
    Banff Centre for Arts and 16
    Canada House Gallery 16
    Quest Gallery 17
    Banff Public Library 18
    Alpine Air Adventures 18
    Banff Adventures 19
    Banff Pedestrian Bridge 19
    Banff Physical Therapy & Massage 20
    Banff Town Sign 20
    Banff Trading Post 21
    Banff Visitor Centre 21
    Banff Visitor Information Kiosk 22
    Bowl Valley | Five Pin & Pints 22
    Eureka Banff Escape Room Adventures 23
    Rocky Mountain Chocolate Banff 23
    Saint Mary Roman Catholic Parish 24
    Tunnel Mountain Summit 24
  Tour Operators Within Banff 25
  Restaurants and Eateries 26

- Accommodations 30
- **LAKE LOUISE** **33**
- **Attractions within the Village of Lake Louise** **34**
  - Lake Louise Visitor Centre 34
  - Moraine Lake 34
  - Lake Agnes 35
  - Peyto Lake 35
  - Morant's Curve 36
  - Fairview Lookout 37
  - Kingmik Dog Sled Tours 37
  - Wild Water Adventures 38
  - Accommodations and Services: 39
- **JASPER** **40**
  - Attractions within Jasper National Park 41
    - Athabasca Falls 41
    - Lac Beauvert 41
    - Maligne Canyon 42
    - Mount Edith Cavell 42
    - Sunwapta Falls 43
    - Valley of the Five Lakes 43
    - Miette Hot Springs 44
    - Sulphur Skyline Trail 44
    - Toe of the Athabasca Glacier Trailhead 46
    - Wilcox Pass Trail 48
    - Tonquin Valley Trail via Astoria Trailhead 50
    - Geraldine Lakes Trail: First Lake 51
    - Jasper SkyTram 53
    - Marmot Basin 54
    - Maligne Lake 55
    - Skyline Trail 56
    - Whistlers Trail 57
  - Campgrounds and Outdoor Living within Jasper National Park 58
- **Attractions within the Town of Jasper** **63**
  - Jasper-Yellowhead Museum & Archives 63
  - Two Brothers Totem Pole 64
  - Jasper Park Information Center 65
  - Mountain Galleries 65
  - Jasper Art Gallery 66
  - Jasper Motorcycle Tours 66
  - Jasper Food Tours 67
  - Maligne Lake Cruise 67
  - Jasper Planetarium & Dark Sky Telescope Tours 68

Rockaboo Mountain Adventures 69
Canadian Skyline Adventures 69
Jasper Hikes and Tours Inc. 70
Jasper Rafting Adventures 70
Jasper Riding Stables 71
Pure Outdoors 71
Maligne Lake Boat House 72
Accommodations and Dining 72

CANMORE 76
Attractions within the Town of Canmore 77
Canmore Museum 77
The Caen More ("Big Head" Sculpture) 77
Canmore Engine Bridge 78
Canmore Nordic Centre 79
Elevation Place 79
Canmore Golf & Curling Club 80
Quarry Lake Park 81
Avens Gallery 81
Carter-Ryan Gallery 82
The Ken Hoehn Gallery 83
Canadian Rockies Earth Science Resource Centre 83
Grassi Lakes 84
Ha Ling Peak Trail 85

Bow Valley Provincial Park - Kananaskis Country 87
Kananaskis Country Conservation Pass 88
Kananaskis Country Summer Events 88
Kananaskis Country Trails 89
Bow River Interpretive 89
Bow Valley Paved 89
Elk Flats 90
Flowing Water Interpretive 90
Heart Creek Interpretive 90
Jewell Pass 90
Many Springs Interpretive 90
Middle Lake Interpretive 91
Montane Interpretive 91
Moraine Interpretive 91
Prairie View 91
Quaite Creek 91
Stoney 92
Adventure and Tours in Canmore 93
YOHO NATIONAL PARK 94

vi

- Village of Field 95
- Emerald Lake 95
- Natural Bridge 95
- Kicking Horse River 96
- Takakkaw Falls 96
- Yoho Valley 96
- Spiral Tunnels viewpoint 97
- Kicking Horse Pass National Historic Site 97
- Wapta Falls 97
- Burgess Shale fossil guided hikes 97
- Sherbrooke Lake Trail 98
- Meeting of the waters confluent 98
- Laughing falls 99
- Additional Services and Facilities 100

ITINERARY **107**
GENERAL INFORMATION **114**

BANFF NATIONAL PARK

Banff National Park, located in the heart of the Canadian Rockies, was formed over millions of years through a series of geological processes including sediment deposition, mountain building, and glacial erosion. The area was originally inhabited by Indigenous peoples including the Stoney Nakoda, Blackfoot, and Tsuut'ina nations, who used the land for hunting and spiritual practices.

The modern history of Banff began in 1883 when three railway workers discovered hot springs on Sulphur Mountain. This discovery led to the creation of Canada's first national park, Banff Hot Springs Reserve, in 1885. The area was expanded and designated as Banff National Park in 1887. The Canadian Pacific Railway played a crucial role in the park's early development, promoting Banff as an international resort and getaway.

In the early 20th century, Banff saw significant development including the construction of the Banff Springs Hotel and the establishment of a comprehensive tourist infrastructure. Over the decades, the park's focus has gradually shifted towards conservation, balancing visitor needs with environmental protection. Today, Banff is known for its stunning landscape, diverse wildlife, and numerous outdoor recreational activities.

Banff Visitor Centre Contact Information
Telephone: +1-403-762-1550
Email: banffinfo@pc.gc.ca
Website: https://parks.canada.ca/pn-np/ab/banff

ATTRACTIONS WITHIN BANFF NATIONAL PARK

Bow Falls and Bow Falls Viewpoint

Location: Bow Falls Ave, Banff, AB T0L 0C0

Admission: Free access to Bow Falls; approximately $8 USD for basic entry to Bow Falls Viewpoint. Multi-attraction passes and guided tours are available for around $17 USD with options for free cancellation.

Description: Bow Falls and Bow Falls Viewpoint are closely situated natural attractions within Banff National Park, Alberta, renowned for their scenic beauty and accessibility. Bow Falls is a wide and short waterfall along the Bow River, set in a valley shaped by ancient glaciers. It offers picturesque views from various vantage points against the backdrop of the Canadian Rockies. The nearby Bow Falls Viewpoint enhances the experience with additional walking and biking trails that provide different perspectives of the falls and surrounding landscapes. The area is equipped with well-maintained pathways, viewing platforms, and facilities such as picnic spots and washrooms, making it ideal for family outings and extended visits. The proximity to the historic Fairmont Banff Springs Hotel makes both locations a convenient and popular stop for hotel guests and other visitors. Both sites are accessible via a short drive from the town of Banff with designated parking areas. The viewpoint is open around the clock, allowing for breathtaking views both day and night. Due to the popularity of these attractions, early morning visits are recommended to avoid crowds, especially during peak tourist seasons.

Bow Falls to Hoodoos Trail

Location: Banff National Park, Alberta

Description: The Hoodoos from Bow Falls Trail offers an immersive 10 km loop journey through the breathtaking landscapes of Banff National Park. This moderately challenging route, with an elevation gain of 280 meters, typically takes about 2 hours and 44 minutes to complete. It is a popular destination for bird watching, mountain biking, snowshoeing, running, and walking, providing ample opportunities to encounter diverse wildlife and scenic views. The trail is accessible to both kids and adults, featuring partially paved paths and forest trails. It includes sections along roads and scenic river vistas, with varied terrain that includes rocky patches and some areas with little shade. Dogs are permitted on the trail but must be kept on a leash. Facilities for parking are available in town, where the trail can be accessed. Seasonal conditions vary; the trail can be icy in winter, making cleats beneficial. Insect repellent is recommended during warmer months due to mosquitoes. Entry to Banff National Park requires a fee, which contributes to the maintenance and preservation of this pristine natural area. Visitors can enjoy a range of experiences from historic sites to wildlife viewing, with the trail providing multiple river access points and lookout areas.

Cave and Basin National Historic Site
Location: 311 Cave Ave, Banff, AB T1L 1K2,
Contact: +1 403-762-1566
Opening Hours:
- Wednesday: Closed
- Thursday to Monday: 11 AM – 5 PM
- Tuesday: Closed

Description: The Cave and Basin National Historic Site is celebrated as the birthplace of Canada's National Parks, showcasing hot mineral springs located within a cave and an emerald-colored outdoor pool. This landmark offers visitors a glimpse into the natural and cultural history of the region, emphasizing the significance of thermal mineral springs in natural park conservation. The site features informative exhibits, a historic bathing pavilion, interactive displays, and the remnants of the original 1880s bathhouse. Accessibility to the site includes pathways and boardwalks suitable for strollers, making it family-friendly. While dogs are allowed on the premises, they must be kept on a leash. Admission is required, costing approximately $9 USD (converted from BGN 11.99), which grants entry to explore the preserved cave and basin. The site is also connected to several trails, such as the Marsh Loop Trailhead, offering more exploration opportunities within Banff National Park.

Visitors can enrich their experience with educational and recreational activities, including guided tours that delve into the geological and social history of the area. Although swimming in the basin is not allowed to protect the local ecosystem, including the endangered Banff Springs snail, the nearby Banff Upper Hot Springs provide an alternative for those wishing to enjoy a thermal water experience. The site is ideal for those interested in geology, history, and the natural scenery of Banff National Park.

Lake Louise Ski Resort & Summer Gondola
Location: 1 Whitehorn Rd, Lake Louise, AB T0L 1E0, Canada
Contact: +1 403-522-3555
Website: www.skilouise.com
Hours: Daily from 8 AM to 5 PM
Description: Lake Louise Ski Resort & Summer Gondola is a premier destination for outdoor enthusiasts, offering a wide array of year-round recreational activities. Situated in the heart of the Canadian Rockies, the resort features expansive ski slopes and a summer gondola ride that provides stunning views of the surrounding mountains and wildlife.

During the winter months, the resort becomes a bustling ski destination with trails suitable for all skill levels, from beginner to expert. The resort is well-known for its well-maintained pistes, diverse terrain including bowls and tree runs, and modern lift systems. Visitors can enjoy skiing, snowboarding, and snowshoe tours among other winter sports. Lift tickets are priced at approximately $30 USD for a single adult, with discounts available for groups.

In the summer, the gondola offers visitors a chance to experience breathtaking panoramic views of Lake Louise and its natural surroundings. The summer activities include guided walks, wildlife viewing, and dining at high altitude, making it a perfect spot for photographers and nature lovers alike.

Dining options at the resort include a variety of eateries such as The Lodge of the Ten Peaks Café, Kuma Yama sushi restaurant, and the Whiskyjack Lodge, catering to different tastes and preferences. The resort is also equipped with rental outlets offering the latest ski and snowboard equipment. Accessibility features include well-paved paths for easy navigation around the resort.

Mount Norquay

Via Ferrata

Sightseeing Chairlift

Cliffhouse Bistro

Banff Eco Transit

Weddings

Plan Your Visit

Season Passes

Snow School

Location: Improvement District No. 9, AB, Canada
Contact: +1 403-762-4421 | **Website:** www.banffnorquay.com
Description: Mount Norquay Ski Resort, located in the scenic Banff National Park, is a premier destination for skiing, tubing, and year-round recreational activities. Offering a diverse range of slopes suitable for all skill levels, the resort is celebrated for its small crowds and minimal waiting times, enhancing the experience for every visitor. Facilities at Mount Norquay include multiple dining options such as the Cliffhouse Bistro and Norquay Lodge, providing excellent meal and relaxation opportunities after a day on the slopes. The resort also hosts a variety of events and activities beyond skiing, including night skiing, biking and a tubing park, making it a versatile attraction for both winter sports enthusiasts and families. Mount Norquay remains a significant attraction within Banff National Park, known for its superb views and quality services. When operational from **June 8, 2024**, visitors are encouraged to explore all that Mount Norquay has to offer, from its well-maintained runs to its comfortable amenities and beautiful mountain vistas.

Parker Ridge

Location: Banff National Park, Improvement District No. 9, Alberta, Canada

Description: Parker Ridge offers a 6.4 km out-and-back hiking trail renowned for its panoramic views and accessibility within Banff National Park. The trail, considered moderately challenging, features an elevation gain of 343 meters and is popular for hiking, snowshoeing, and running. Visitors are drawn to this trail for its stunning vistas of the Saskatchewan Glacier and the expansive glacial valley. Starting just south of the Athabasca Glacier Visitors Center, which provides ample parking and restroom facilities, the hike begins with a series of switchbacks through a forested area, leading to open views across the valley. The area, known for its delicate alpine

ecosystem, requires visitors to stay on designated paths to preserve the environment. While the trail typically concludes at the ridge, adventurous hikers can extend their journey by exploring the rocky ridge towards Mount Athabasca. The trailhead is easily accessible via the Icefields Parkway at KM 117, approximately 4 km south of the Banff-Jasper boundary, offering a fulfilling adventure for those seeking to experience the natural beauty of the Canadian Rockies.

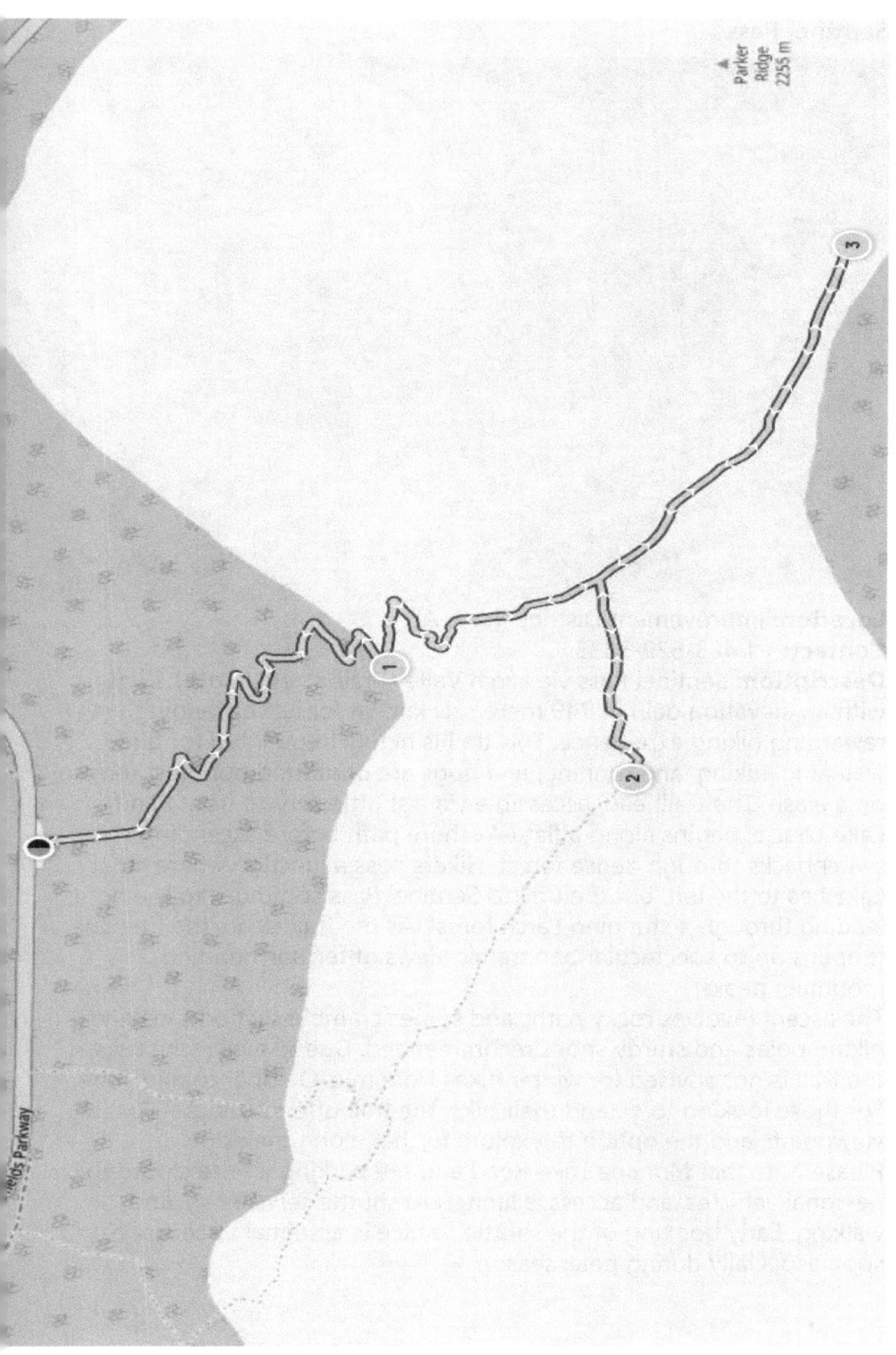

Sentinel Pass

Location: Improvement District No. 9, AB
Contact: +1 403-522-3833
Description: Sentinel Pass via Larch Valley Trail, stretching 11.1 km with an elevation gain of 749 meters, is known for its challenging yet rewarding hiking experience. This trail is highly frequented for bird watching, hiking, and running, and dogs are permitted but must remain on a leash. The trailhead, accessible via a shuttle service from Banff or Lake Louise, begins along a flat lakeshore path before ascending steep switchbacks through dense forest. Hikers pass a junction where Eiffel Lake lies to the left, but the trail to Sentinel Pass continues to the right, leading through a stunning Larch forest. As the trail clears the tree line, it opens up to spectacular panoramic views of ten surrounding mountain peaks.
The ascent involves rocky paths and some scramble sections, making hiking poles and sturdy shoes recommended. Due to avalanche risks, the trail is not advised for winter hikes from mid-October to mid-June. For those looking to extend their hike, the trail offers multiple viewpoints and the option to explore further along the ridge.
Please note that Moraine Lake Road and the parking lot are closed to personal vehicles, and access is limited to shuttle services, cycling, or walking. Early booking of the shuttle service is essential to secure a spot, especially during peak season.

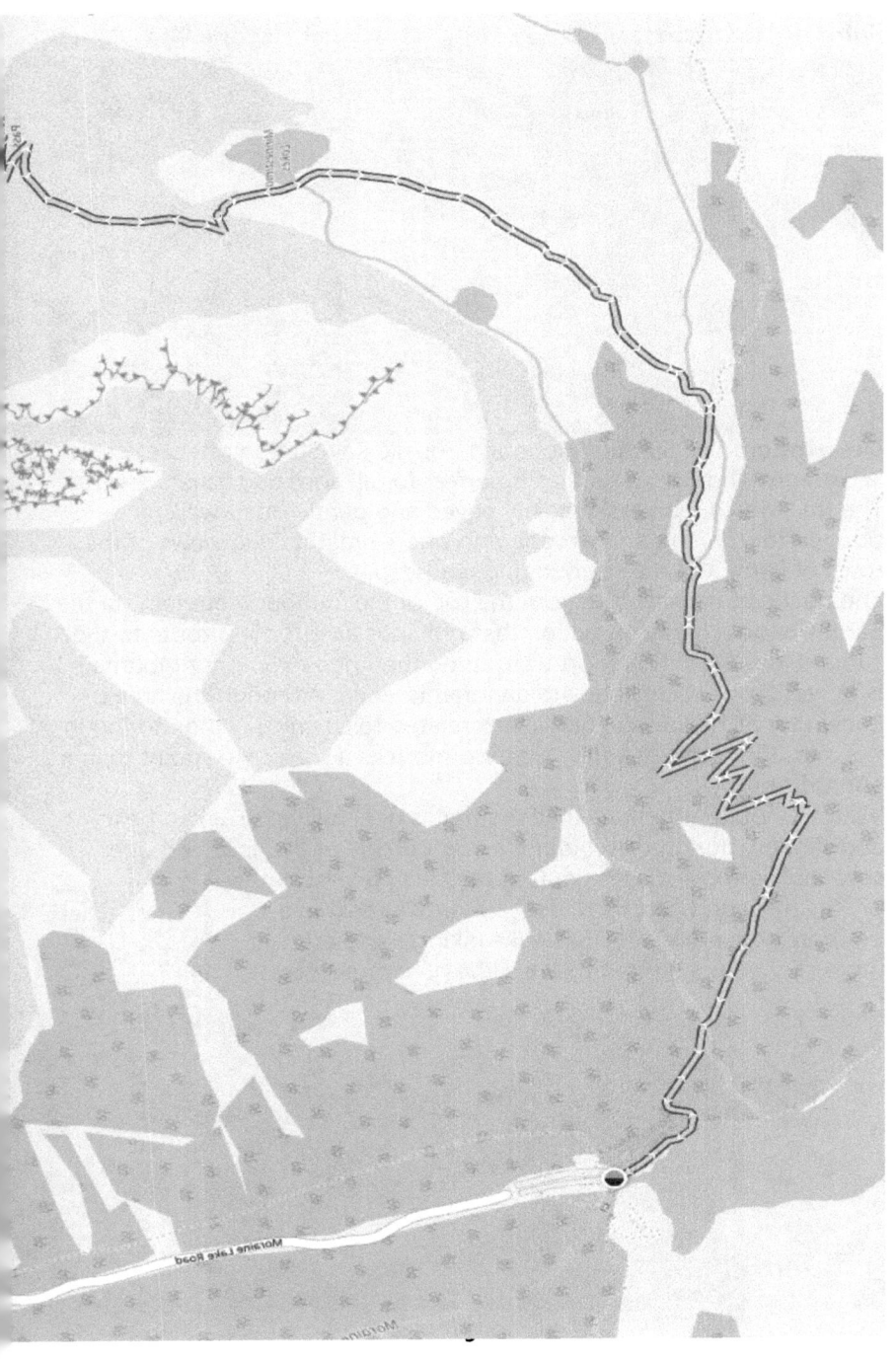

Sulphur Mountain Cosmic Ray Station National Historic Site

Description: The Sulphur Mountain Cosmic Ray Station offers a scenic 1.1 km out-and-back trail that is perfect for all ages and fitness levels. The trail, which features a mostly paved and gentle boardwalk, is popular for running and walking and offers breathtaking views of the town of Banff and the surrounding landscapes.

The trailhead is accessible from the top of the Sulphur Mountain via the Banff Gondola, a key attraction that provides an effortless route to the summit and back. This short walk along the ridge of Sulphur Mountain is famed for its accessible and panoramic views. Although the area is known for its historical significance related to cosmic ray monitoring in the mid-20th century, today it serves more as a scenic viewpoint than a scientific outpost.

Visitors should note that while the trail is generally easy, it can be icy and slippery during the colder months outside of the specified open season. Therefore, visiting during the clear, dry months of May through October is ideal. For those seeking a bit more adventure, an alternative hiking route offers a more challenging ascent to the same panoramic views.

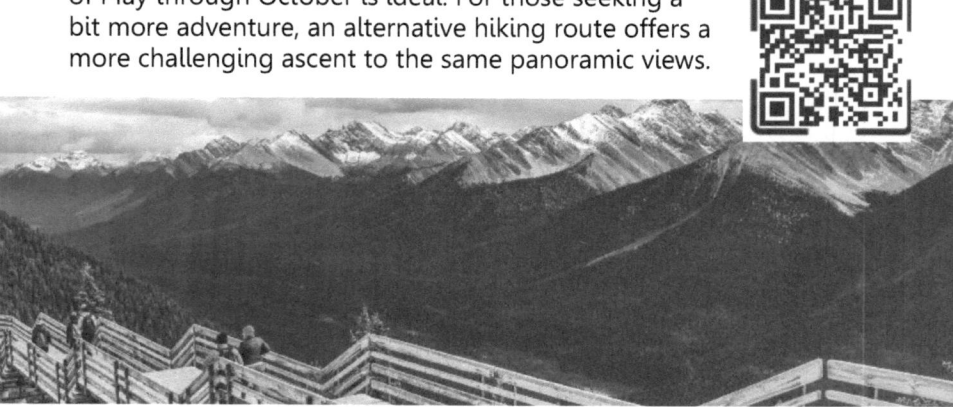

Sundance Canyon
Location: Vermilion Lakes Rd, Improvement District No. 9, AB T0L 2C0, Canada
Description: Sundance Canyon, nestled in the scenic surroundings of Banff National Park, offers a family-friendly hiking experience accessible to visitors of all ages. The main trail is a 3.9 km paved path starting at the historic Cave and Basin site, winding through beautiful natural landscapes and leading to a series of picturesque waterfalls. This trail is perfect for both walking and biking, offering ample opportunities to enjoy the great outdoors while maintaining social distancing. The canyon is not only known for its accessible trails but also for its rich natural environment, where wildlife sightings, including bears, are common, adding an element of adventure to every visit. The trail culminates in the real canyon area, which visitors are encouraged to explore beyond the initial picnic areas to fully appreciate its beauty. Sundance Canyon remains open 24 hours, allowing for flexible visitation times, though it is most popular during daylight hours for safety and visibility.

Surprise Corner Viewpoint

Location: Buffalo St, Banff, AB T1L 1K2, Canada
Contact: +1 403-762-1550 | **Website:** www.pc.gc.ca
Description: Surprise Corner Viewpoint offers a scenic overlook of the historic 1888 Fairmont Banff Springs Hotel and Sulphur Mountain. This popular spot in Banff provides visitors

with one of the most iconic views in the area, making it a must-visit destination for photographers and sightseers alike. The viewpoint provides stunning views at sunrise, sunset, and even under starlit skies. Visitors can enjoy the breathtaking scenery from a well-constructed observation deck, which ensures unobstructed views of the surrounding mountains and the architectural elegance of the Fairmont Banff Springs. The site has a small parking area, which can become crowded during peak times, so arriving early or visiting during off-peak hours is recommended. The Surprise Corner Viewpoint is not only a fantastic place to start a hike but also a peaceful spot to relax and take in the beauty of Banff National Park.

The Fenlands Banff Recreation Centre

Location: 100 Mt Norquay Rd #2F, Banff, AB T1L 1C3, Canada
Contact: +1 403-762-1235
Hours: Daily, 8:30AM - 8:30 PM
Description: The Fenlands Banff Recreation Centre is a premier facility located in the heart of Banff, providing a variety of recreational and fitness options. This center offers amenities such as an ice rink for hockey and skating, curling facilities, and spaces for public events and tournaments. The facility is known for its friendly staff, clean environment, and the variety of programs available to both locals and visitors. The recreation center is easily accessible, featuring good parking options and robust wifi connectivity, making it a convenient location for families and individuals looking to engage in sports or recreational activities. The outdoor skating loop is a highlight during the winter months, offering a unique skating experience amidst beautiful natural surroundings. Visitors are encouraged to bring their own equipment to enjoy the full range of activities available at this well-equipped recreation center.

Don't miss the opportunity to experience this exceptional recreational hub. Plan your visit now, check out the variety of programs offered, and make the most of the outstanding facilities available at The Fenlands Banff Recreation Centre. Whether you're looking to join a fitness class, skate on the outdoor loop, or try your hand at curling, The Fenlands provides a welcoming environment for all ages and skill levels. Make your visit a priority for a fun and engaging day out in Banff!

Lake Louise Sport & Recreation
Location: 103 Village Rd, Lake Louise, AB
Contact: +1 403-522-2606
Website: www.improvementdistrict9.ca
Description: The Lake Louise Sport & Recreation Centre is a versatile facility located in the stunning setting of Lake Louise, Alberta. This recreation center boasts a range of activities suitable for all seasons, from ice skating in the winter to roller skating in the summer. The center is equipped with heated change rooms, making it comfortable for visitors even in the colder months. The outdoor rink provides a great surface for various sports and is complemented by a roof that protects while still allowing the natural elements to enhance the experience. This center is celebrated for its beautiful location and the array of amenities it packs into a compact area, making it a cherished spot among locals and tourists alike.

ATTRACTIONS WITHIN THE TOWN OF BANFF

Banff Park Museum National Historic Site
Location: 91 Banff Ave, Banff, AB T1L 1K2
Contact: +1 403-762-1558
Hours: Saturday and Sunday: 11 AM – 5 PM; Closed Monday to Friday
Description: The Banff Park Museum National Historic Site, housed in a landmark 1903 building, serves as a window into the natural history of the region. This museum, recognized as a National Historic Site, features a wide range of educational exhibits focusing on the flora and fauna of Banff National Park. Its collection includes an extensive array of taxidermy and natural specimens, providing visitors with a detailed look at the wildlife indigenous to the area. The museum is a treasure trove for those interested in natural science and the preservation of Canadian wildlife. Visitors can enjoy the museum's offerings on weekends, with free entry on select days and multilingual tours available to enhance the educational experience. As the museum operates on a seasonal schedule with limited weekend hours, planning your visit in advance is advisable to make the most of this enriching cultural attraction.

Buffalo Nations Museum

Location: 1 Birch Ave, Banff, AB T1L 1A8, Canada
Contact: +1 403-762-2388
Website: www.buffalonationsmuseum.com
Opening Hours: Daily 10 AM – 6 PM
Description: The Buffalo Nations Museum is a fort-like structure dedicated to showcasing the history and culture of the local Indigenous Canadians. Located in Banff, this museum presents a comprehensive collection of artifacts, including traditional clothing, tools, and art, which provide insight into the lives and traditions of First Nations peoples. The museum's exhibits are designed to educate visitors about the significant contributions and rich cultural heritage of Indigenous communities in the region.

The museum is open every day, offering guests the opportunity to explore extensive exhibits at their own pace. It includes a gift shop that features a range of unique, culturally significant items, allowing visitors to take a piece of Indigenous artistry home with them.

Historic Luxton Home Museum

Location: 206 Beaver St, Banff, AB T1L 1B4, Canada
Contact: +1 403-762-2105
Website: www.luxtonfoundation.org
Opening Hours: Thursday to Sunday: 10 AM – 4 PM; Closed Monday to Wednesday
Description: The Historic Luxton Home Museum is set in the 1905 residence of the Luxton family, prominent figures in the history of Banff. This museum showcases a rich collection of antiques and offers a glimpse into the early 20th-century lifestyle of the Luxtons. Visitors to the museum can explore vibrant gardens and a well-preserved home that reflects the family's significant influence on the cultural and social fabric of Banff.

The museum operates on a seasonal schedule, with regular hours for the public from Thursday to Sunday, and is closed from Monday to

Wednesday. It provides a unique educational experience, highlighting the historical narrative of Banff through the personal history of the Luxton family. This site not only serves as a historical museum but also acts as a cultural hub that preserves and interprets the legacy of a family instrumental in the development of the community.

Whyte Museum of the Canadian Rockies
Location: 111 Bear St, Banff, AB T1L 1A3, Canada
Contact: +1 403-762-2291
Website: www.whyte.org
Opening Hours: Daily 10 AM – 5 PM
Description: The Whyte Museum of the Canadian Rockies in Banff provides an extensive exploration of the region's cultural heritage and natural history through its exhibits. The museum showcases a collection of landscape paintings, preserved early Banff homes and cabins, and various heritage exhibits that tell the story of the Rockies and its inhabitants. The museum's archives offer a treasure trove of art, artifacts, and photographs, presenting a detailed narrative of the area's historical and environmental evolution. Visitors can engage with interactive listening options throughout the exhibitions, which are included in the museum entry. Although there is no audio guide, the museum has developed an app to enhance visitor experience.

Art Of Man Gallery
Location: 111 Lake Louise Dr, Lake Louise, AB T0L 1E0, Canada (Floor 1 · Fairmont Château Lake Louise)
Contact: +1 403-522-3684
Opening Hours: Saturday: 12 PM – 8 PM, Sunday: 10 AM – 6:30 PM, Monday to Friday: 11 AM – 7 PM
Description: The Art Of Man Gallery is located within the prestigious Fairmont Château Lake Louise, offering a unique collection of artworks with a focus on Aboriginal cultures. This gallery provides visitors a chance to explore a diverse range of artistic

expressions, prominently featuring sculptures and paintings that celebrate various aspects of indigenous heritage.

The gallery operates daily with varying hours, providing ample opportunity for visitors to experience its offerings. While the gallery has been noted for its rich array of art, it has received mixed reviews regarding customer service and the authenticity of some pieces. Visitors are encouraged to engage with the artworks and form their own opinions on the cultural representations on display.

Banff Centre for Arts and Creativity
Location: 107 Tunnel Mountain Dr, Banff, AB T1L 1H5, Canada
Contact: +1 403-762-6100
Website: www.banffcentre.ca
Opening Hours: Open 24 hours
Description: The Banff Centre for Arts and Creativity is a globally renowned institution dedicated to the development of arts and culture. Situated in the scenic environment of Banff National Park, the center offers a variety of programs and facilities aimed at fostering creativity and innovation in the arts. Visitors can experience an array of performances, exhibitions, and workshops facilitated by talented artists and creative thinkers from around the world.

The campus features modern amenities, including the Maclab Bistro, Three Ravens Restaurant & Wine Bar, Sally Borden Fitness and Recreation, and Vistas Dining Hall, enhancing the visitor experience with culinary delights and recreational options.

Canada House Gallery
Location: 201 Bear St, Banff, AB T1L 1B5, Canada
Contact: +1 403-762-3757
Website: www.canadahouse.com
Opening Hours: Monday to Thursday and Sunday: 10 AM – 5 PM; Friday and Saturday: 10 AM – 7 PM
Description: Established in 1974, Canada House Gallery is a prominent art gallery located in Banff, showcasing a curated collection of contemporary local art, sculpture, and native crafts. The gallery is

known for its engaging display of works from a diverse array of Canadian artists, offering visitors a glimpse into Canada's vibrant artistic landscape. The atmosphere is low-key, allowing for a personal and intimate exploration of the art.

Visitors can expect to find a range of artworks that celebrate the rich cultural and natural heritage of the region. The gallery is staffed by knowledgeable and passionate individuals who are eager to discuss the art and artists featured. Although the art pieces can be on the pricier side, the gallery provides a window into the high quality and uniqueness of Canadian artistry.

Quest Gallery
Location: Fairmont Banff Springs, 405 Spray Ave, Banff, AB T1L 1J4, Canada
Contact: +1 403-762-4422
Website: www.thequestgallery.com
Opening Hours: Monday to Tuesday and Sunday: 9 AM – 6 PM; Wednesday to Thursday: 9 AM – 8 PM; Friday to Saturday: 9 AM – 9 PM

Description: The Quest Gallery, located within the iconic Fairmont Banff Springs, is an art gallery celebrated for its exceptional selection of fine art. This gallery offers a diverse range of artworks, from intricate sculptures to exquisite paintings, all curated to reflect the unique cultural and natural beauty of the Canadian Rockies. Visitors to The Quest Gallery are treated to a visual feast that often includes local and international pieces, making it a must-visit destination for art enthusiasts staying at or visiting the Fairmont Banff Springs.

The gallery's highly rated customer service and the quality of its art pieces make it a standout attraction in Banff. With flexible opening hours and a convenient location, The Quest Gallery provides a perfect opportunity for guests to explore art in a luxurious setting. Whether you are looking to purchase a piece or simply appreciate the fine works on display, The Quest Gallery ensures a memorable and enriching experience.

Banff Public Library
Location: 101 Bear St, Banff, AB T1L 1H3, Canada
Contact: +1 403-762-2661
Website: www.banfflibrary.ab.ca
Opening Hours:
- Monday to Thursday: 10 AM – 7 PM
- Friday: 10 AM – 6 PM
- Saturday and Sunday: 11 AM – 5 PM

Description: Banff Public Library offers a tranquil retreat from the bustling streets of Banff, providing a comprehensive range of services and resources for both locals and visitors. This library is well-loved for its inviting atmosphere and extensive selection of materials, including books, DVDs, and a special collection known as the 'Library of Things'. It boasts comfortable seating areas equipped with power outlets for those with laptops, and a vibrant children's section that makes it a family-friendly destination. The library is also equipped with public computers, free Wi-Fi, and offers printing services in multiple languages, catering to the needs of a diverse community. Regularly scheduled closures for holidays such as Good Friday and Easter Monday are noted, and patrons are reminded to return borrowed items using the convenient book drop or directly at the front desk for special items.

Alpine Air Adventures
Location: 229 Bear St #14, Banff, AB T1L 1B5, Canada
Contact: +1 403-522-2700
Website: www.alpineairadventures.com
Opening Hours: Daily 8 AM – 6 PM
Description: Alpine Air Adventures offers an array of exhilarating outdoor activities centered around adventure sports in the stunning landscape of Banff, Canada. With activities ranging from introductory backcountry skiing to comprehensive ice climbing sessions, the company caters to thrill-seekers of various skill levels. Highly experienced guides ensure safety while navigating challenging terrains or assessing avalanche risks, tailoring each adventure to current conditions and client capabilities. The headquarters are conveniently located near central Banff, providing

easy access to the vast natural playground surrounding the area. Booking in advance is recommended, ensuring a personalized and fulfilling adventure experience.

Banff Adventures
Location: 211 Bear St #104, Banff, AB T1L 1A8, Canada
Contact: +1 403-762-4554
Website: www.banffadventures.com
Opening Hours: Daily 8:30 AM – 7 PM
Description: Banff Adventures operates as a premier outdoor activity organizer based in Banff, Alberta, offering a vast array of guided tours and experiences tailored to adventure seekers. From serene walks at the Yamnuska Wolfdog Sanctuary to thrilling excursions across the Columbia Icefield Skywalk, and the picturesque Golden Skybridge, this organizer provides a comprehensive suite of options to explore the natural splendor of the region. Each activity is designed to accommodate various levels of adventure and provides instant confirmations for ease of planning. Banff Adventures' location in central Banff makes it an easily accessible starting point for tourists looking to explore the Canadian Rockies. Advance booking via their official website ensures a seamless and enriched outdoor experience.

Banff Pedestrian Bridge
Location: Bow River, Banff, AB, Canada
Description: The Banff Pedestrian Bridge, located over the Bow River in Banff, Alberta, provides a picturesque pathway for pedestrians to enjoy stunning views of the surrounding landscapes. This bridge is a favorite spot for both locals and tourists, offering a scenic route that connects various points of interest along the river. It is particularly popular for its accessibility and the opportunity it offers for photography, scenic walks, and

peaceful reflection. The bridge enhances the charm of Banff, making it a must-visit destination for those seeking to experience the natural beauty of the area. Visitors can access the bridge at any time, as it is open 24 hours a day, ensuring that the breathtaking views of the river and mountains can be enjoyed both during the day and at night.

Banff Physical Therapy & Massage
Location: 220 Bear St, Banff, AB T1L 1C3, Canada (Located in: Bear Street Mall)
Contact: +1 403-762-3734 |
Website: www.banffphysicaltherapy.com
Hours: Monday to Friday: 7 AM – 7 PM | Saturday: 7 AM – 12 PM | Closed on Sun

Description: Banff Physical Therapy & Massage offers a comprehensive range of physiotherapy and massage services aimed at treating injuries, enhancing physical health, and promoting overall wellness. Situated within the Bear Street Mall in Banff, Alberta, the clinic is renowned for its expert team of therapists who provide personalized treatment plans. Services include manual therapy, injury rehabilitation, custom exercise programs, and various massage techniques, all tailored to meet individual needs. The clinic is a vital resource for both locals and visitors seeking professional physical therapy and massage services in a supportive and healing environment.

Banff Town Sign
Location: 101 Mt Norquay Rd, Banff, AB T1L 1C3, Canada
Contact: +1 403-762-8421
Website: Not available
Opening Hours: Open 24 hours
Description: The Banff Town Sign is a prominent landmark located at the gateway to the picturesque town of Banff, Alberta. This sign is not just a popular photo spot but also serves as a welcoming point for visitors entering the town. Positioned along Mt. Norquay Road, it offers a backdrop of stunning mountain scenery, making it an

ideal location for memorable photographs. The sign is accessible round the clock and there is no fee for visiting. It is conveniently situated with available parking facilities nearby, ensuring easy access for all visitors looking to capture a piece of Banff's charm.

Banff Trading Post

Location: 101 Cave Ave, Banff, AB T1L 1A9, Canada
Contact: +1 403-762-2456
Website: www.bansftradingpost.com
Opening Hours: Monday to Saturday 10 AM – 6 PM; Closed on Sundays
Description: Banff Trading Post is a unique retail destination offering a diverse selection of Native American goods. This store, situated in the Bear Street Mall, provides visitors with an array of indigenous arts and crafts, including handmade art, dream catchers, clothing, shoes, mugs, and more. The store is known for its eclectic mix of items, with standout pieces like the famed Merman and other curiosities. It serves as a cultural hub in Banff, offering both locals and tourists a chance to purchase authentic, locally-sourced indigenous products.

Banff Visitor Centre

Location: 224 Banff Ave, Banff, AB T1L 1B3, Canada
Contact: +1 403-762-8421
Website: www.banfflakelouise.com
Hours: Daily from 9 AM to 5 PM
Description: The Banff Visitor Centre is centrally located in Banff National Park and serves as a primary resource for tourists seeking information on the region's extensive recreational opportunities and attractions. The center provides visitors with detailed maps, trail guides, and expert advice on exploring the surrounding area. Additionally, the visitor center houses a souvenir shop offering a variety of local crafts, books, and other memorabilia ideal for gifts or personal keepsakes. Information on weather conditions, safety tips, and park

regulations are also available, ensuring visitors can plan their activities safely and effectively. Conveniently, the visitor center is also home to the Bow Valley Regional Transit Services Commission, offering public transportation information and services directly from the premises.

Banff Visitor Information Kiosk
Location: 327 Railway Ave, Banff, AB T1L 1A9, Canada
Contact: +1 403-762-8421 | **Website:** www.banfflakelouise.com
Opening Hours: Daily from 9 AM to 5 PM
Description: The Banff Visitor Information Kiosk, strategically located at the Banff Heritage Railway Station, serves as a pivotal resource for visitors to the area. It offers essential information on regional hikes, parks, and other activities, and facilitates the purchase of park passes. Amenities include maps, tour booking assistance, and expert local advice, ensuring visitors can fully engage with the wealth of natural beauty and outdoor opportunities Banff has to offer. Additional services at the kiosk include bike and scooter rentals, allowing for an enhanced exploration of the surrounding landscape.

Bowl Valley | Five Pin & Pints
Location: 405 Spray Ave, Banff, AB T1L 1J9, Canada
Contact: +1 403-762-6892
Website: www.banff-springs-hotel.com
Opening Hours:
- Monday to Friday: 4 PM – 11 PM
- Saturday and Sunday: 11 AM – 11 PM

Description: Located on the first floor of the iconic Fairmont Banff Springs, Bowl Valley | Five Pin & Pints offers a unique and modern bowling experience in the heart of Banff. This intimate venue features five-pin bowling in a cozy yet vibrant setting, ideal for both families and friends looking for entertainment. The facility is noted for its friendly atmosphere, quality food options, and a selection of drinks. While it may be on the pricier side, guests enjoy top-notch service and a memorable experience.

Eureka Banff Escape Room Adventures
Location: 229 Bear St, Banff, AB T1L 1C3, Canada
Contact: +1 403-762-8612
Website: www.eurekabanff.com
Opening Hours: Sunday to Thursday: 12 PM – 10 PM, Friday: 12:15 PM – 10 PM, Saturday: 12 PM – 10 PM

Description: Eureka Banff Escape Room Adventures is a popular amusement center located in Banff, offering uniquely themed escape rooms that challenge participants with puzzles and clues to enhance their experience in the heart of the Rockies. The facility provides a range of themed rooms suitable for family outings, group activities, or team-building events. Each room is meticulously designed with attention to detail, offering immersive scenarios that include a 1950s diner and the Warden's Room for varying difficulty levels. The center is well-regarded for its creative setups and friendly staff, making it an excellent choice for those looking for interactive entertainment in Banff. Advanced bookings are recommended to secure a spot, especially during peak tourist seasons.

Rocky Mountain Chocolate Banff
Location: 117B Banff Ave, Banff, AB T1L 1C1, Canada
Contact: +1 403-985-0987
Website: www.rockychoc.com
Opening Hours:
Sunday to Thursday: 11 AM – 8 PM
Friday and Saturday: 11 AM – 9 PM

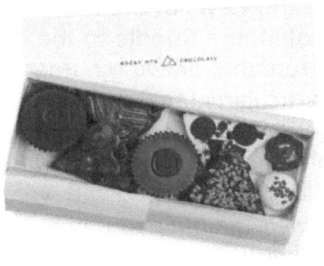

Rocky Mtn Chocolate Banff is a chocolate shop known for its premium chocolates and a variety of confections including cocoa and gift baskets. This retailer is renowned for its array of handmade chocolate treats and offers services such as takeaway and no-contact delivery. Conveniently located on Banff Ave, it provides a sweet spot for both locals and tourists looking to indulge or purchase gifts.

Saint Mary Roman Catholic Parish
Location: 305 Squirrel St, Banff, AB T1L 1B1, Canada
Contact: +1 403-762-3450
Website: www.stmarysparishbanff.ca
Opening Hours:
- Sunday: 9 AM – 12 PM
- Monday to Friday: 10 AM – 4 PM
- Saturday: 4 PM – 6:30 PM

Description: Saint Mary Roman Catholic Parish in Banff provides a serene and welcoming space for worship and community engagement. Located on Squirrel Street, this church caters to both the local community and visitors with regular services and special events. The parish features distinctive architecture that incorporates local cultural elements, offering a peaceful environment for reflection and worship.

Tunnel Mountain Summit
Location: Improvement District No. 9, AB T0L 2C0, Canada
Description: Tunnel Mountain Summit provides a moderately challenging hike accessible directly from downtown Banff. This 4.3 km out-and-back trail, with an elevation gain of 262 meters, offers stunning views of the town of Banff, the Bow Valley, and the dramatic rise of Mount Rundle to the south. It is a favored spot for both hiking and running, drawing numerous visitors throughout the year. This trail is particularly family-friendly and can be enjoyed by hikers of various experience levels. While dogs are allowed, they must be kept on a leash at all times in compliance with Banff National Park's regulations. The trail is also equipped with various amenities, including clear signage and well-maintained paths, ensuring a safe and enjoyable experience for all visitors.

Due to its proximity to wildlife habitats, visitors during the elk calving season from May 15 to June 30 should exercise additional caution. Elk mothers are known to protect their young aggressively. In addition to the natural beauty and recreational opportunities, the trail offers educational content about the local ecology and geology, making it an enriching experience for all. The mountain boasts stunning vistas, including panoramic views of Banff town, Glacier Lake, and Sulphur Mountain, making it a must-visit destination for nature lovers and hikers alike.

Tour Operators Within Banff

Discover Banff Tours
Location: 215 Banff Ave, Banff, AB T1L 1C1, Canada
Contact: +1 877-565-9372 | **Website:** www.banfftours.com
Opening Hours: Open daily from 7:30 AM to 8:00 PM.
Description: Discover Banff Tours is a sightseeing tour agency located on the first floor of Sundance Mall in Banff, offering a wide range of guided tours that showcase the breathtaking natural beauty and diverse wildlife of Banff National Park. From leisurely sightseeing excursions to Lake Louise to adventurous snowshoeing tours, and even unique experiences like the Paranormal History Walking Ghost Tour, Discover Banff Tours provides a variety of options suitable for all ages. The tours emphasize family-friendly activities, ensuring that even the youngest visitors can appreciate the splendor of the park. Visitors can book tours directly through their website, with options available for every season, catering to a range of interests and preferences.

Hop On Banff Ltd.
Location: 211 Bear St, Banff, AB T1L 1A8, Canada
Contact: +1 403-609-5242
Website: www.hoponbanff.com
Opening Hours: Daily 7:00 AM – 7:00 PM
Description: Hop On Banff Ltd. is a tour operator based in Banff, providing flexible sightseeing options across Banff National Park. The service operates a hop-on hop-off bus system that offers a convenient way for visitors to explore major attractions at their own pace. Starting from Banff, the route covers various key sights, including Moraine Lake and other popular landmarks, with the flexibility to spend as much or as little time at each location as desired. This service is especially popular among those who wish to avoid the hassle of parking in busy tourist spots. Advanced booking is advised to ensure availability, particularly during peak tourist seasons.

Open Top Touring
Location: 138 Banff Ave, Banff, AB T1L 1A7, Canada
Contact: +1 877-258-6877
Website: www.opentoptouring.com
Opening Hours: Daily from 9 AM to 6 PM
Description: Open Top Touring offers a distinctive sightseeing experience in Banff, Alberta, with their unique, open-top tour vehicles.

Situated within the Town Centre Mall, this tour operator specializes in guided excursions that showcase Banff's rich history and stunning landscapes. Their offerings include the "Banff Hot Springs and Trails GPS-Guided Walking Tour" and the comprehensive "Legendary Banff Tour," among others, providing instant confirmation and mobile ticket options for convenience. This service caters to those seeking an immersive exploration of Banff's natural and historical treasures.

Restaurants and Eateries

A&W Canada

Location: Husky Gas Station, 601 Banff Ave, Banff, AB T1L 1A2
Contact: +1 403-762-0465
Website: www.aw.ca
Opening Hours: Monday to Thursday, Sunday: 6 AM – 1 AM
- Friday to Saturday: 6 AM – 2 AM
Description: A&W Canada in Banff is a fast-food outlet known for serving its signature root beer, along with a variety of burgers, chicken, and fries. Located within the Husky Gas Station on Banff Avenue, this restaurant offers convenient dining options such as dine-in, kerbside pickup, and delivery. A&W is particularly popular for providing an early breakfast and late-night dining options, catering to both early risers and late-night cravings.

BeaverTails Banff (East)

Location: 120 Banff Ave, Banff, AB T1L 1E7, Canada
Contact: +1 403-985-0086
Website: www.beavertails.com
Opening Hours: Monday to Friday: 12 PM – 9 PM
- Saturday and Sunday: 11 AM – 10 PM
Description: BeaverTails Banff (East) is a popular fast food restaurant known for its unique and delicious BeaverTails - a fried dough pastry, individually hand stretched to resemble a beaver's tail. Located on Banff Avenue, this eatery offers a variety of toppings from classic cinnamon sugar to the decadent chocolate hazelnut.
The restaurant is celebrated for its comfort food, particularly the sweet and savory BeaverTails and Pouttail - a delightful combination of poutine served on a BeaverTail. Visitors often praise the establishment for its tasty treats that serve as perfect snacks after a day of exploring Banff.

Block Kitchen + Bar
Location: 5 Banff Ave #201, Banff, AB T1L 1C6, Canada
(Floor 1 · Town Centre Mall)
Contact: +1 403-985-2887
Website: www.banffblock.com
Opening Hours: Daily 11:30 AM – 10 PM
Description: Block Kitchen + Bar in Banff offers an eclectic menu of small plates with an Asian flair, served in a hip, convivial atmosphere. Located centrally on Banff Avenue, this restaurant is known for its innovative approach to dining, combining the casual tapas style with bold Asian flavors, resulting in a vibrant and unique culinary experience.
Guests can enjoy a variety of dishes such as oysters, curry ramen, salmon poke, and unique desserts like tiramisu, all crafted with a creative twist. The restaurant also offers a selection of wine and cocktails, making it a popular spot for both dining and social gatherings.

Boston Pizza
Location: 225 Banff Ave #201, Banff, AB T1L 1A2, Canada
Contact: +1 403-762-2192
Website: www.bostonpizza.com
Opening Hours:
- Sunday to Thursday: 11 AM – 10 PM
- Friday and Saturday: 11 AM – 12 AM

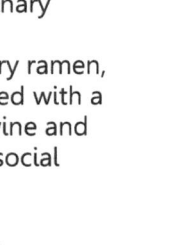

Description: Boston Pizza in Banff offers a familiar and relaxed dining experience with a diverse menu that includes a variety of pizzas, pasta dishes, and a selection of American and Italian cuisine. Located on Banff Avenue, this restaurant is a convenient and popular choice for both locals and tourists seeking a casual dining spot. Boston Pizza is known for its family-friendly atmosphere and sports-friendly vibe, often hosting sports events on their screens which makes it a go-to place for game nights. Besides dine-in, they offer kerbside pickup and no-contact delivery, ensuring that guests have multiple dining options.

Chili's Grill & Bar
Location: 461 Banff Ave, Banff, AB T1L 1B1, Canada
(Located in: Fox Hotel & Suites)
Contact: +1 403-760-8502
Website: www.chilis.com
Opening Hours:
- Monday to Thursday, Sunday: 7 AM – 10 PM
- Friday and Saturday: 7 AM – 11 PM

Description: Chili's Grill & Bar in Banff offers a family-friendly dining experience with a menu that features classic Tex-Mex and American fare. Set in a Southwestern-style atmosphere, this restaurant is known for its hearty meals that include favorites such as burgers, fajitas, and a variety of appetizers.
Chili's provides multiple dining options including dine-in, takeaway, and no-contact delivery, accommodating all dining preferences.

COWS Banff
Location: 138 Banff Ave Unit #111, Banff, AB T1L 1C3, Canada (Located in: Mount Royal Hotel)
Contact: +1 403-760-3493
Website: www.cows.ca
Opening Hours: Daily 11 AM – 9 PM
Description: COWS Banff is an iconic ice cream shop known for its premium, super creamy ice cream and a whimsical array of cow-themed merchandise. Situated in the heart of Banff, this store offers a delightful experience with its fun and creatively named ice cream flavors, ranging from classic to unique local blends.
Visitors can enjoy their ice cream in freshly made waffle cones, surrounded by a playful and inviting atmosphere that often features cow puns and humorous decor. COWS Banff is also famous for its high-quality ingredients, ensuring each scoop is a rich and satisfying treat. Alongside ice cream, the shop sells a variety of fun merchandise, including t-shirts and novelty items, making it a must-visit for both ice cream lovers and those looking for unique souvenirs from Banff.

Good Earth Coffeehouse

Location: 333 Banff Ave, Banff, AB T1L 1B1, Canada (Located in: Elk + Avenue Hotel)
Contact: +1 403-985-0989
Website: www.goodearthcoffeehouse.com
Opening Hours: Daily 6:30 AM – 7 PM
Description: Good Earth Coffeehouse in Banff offers a cozy, inviting space for coffee lovers and food enthusiasts alike. This informal counter-serve cafe, situated within the Elk + Avenue Hotel on Banff Avenue, provides a range of espresso drinks, freshly baked goods, smoothies, and hearty sandwiches. The coffeehouse is well-known for its welcoming patio area, where guests can enjoy their beverages and meals outdoors with a view of the surrounding mountainous landscape. With its commitment to quality and community, Good Earth Coffeehouse serves as a popular spot for both locals and tourists seeking a relaxing atmosphere and delicious offerings.

The Keg Steakhouse + Bar

Location: 117 Banff Ave, Banff, AB T1L 1A4, Canada
Contact: +1 403-760-3030
Website: www.thekeg.com
Opening Hours:
- Monday to Thursday: 4 PM – 9 PM
- Friday: 4 PM – 9 PM
- Saturday to Sunday: 3 PM – 9 PM

Description: The Keg Steakhouse + Bar in Banff Downtown offers a polished yet relaxed dining atmosphere, specializing in classic steak and seafood dishes. This location provides a stylish setting perfect for both casual dinners and special occasions. Known for its high-quality meals and excellent service, the restaurant features a full bar with a wide selection of wines and cocktails. Guests can also enjoy the convenience of both dine-in and takeout options, including kerbside pickup and delivery.

The Old Spaghetti Factory (Banff)

Location: Cascade Shops, F2, 317 Banff Ave, Banff, AB T1L 1C1, Canada
Contact: +1 403-760-2779
Website: www.oldspaghettifactory.ca
Opening Hours:
- Sunday to Wednesday: 11:30 AM – 9 PM
- Thursday to Saturday: 11:30 AM – 10 PM

Description: Located in the Cascade Shops, The Old Spaghetti Factory in Banff offers a family-friendly dining experience, featuring traditional Italian dishes in a unique turn-of-the-century atmosphere. This popular chain restaurant is known for providing value with all meals including a starter of bread, soup or salad, coffee or tea, and ice cream. The menu boasts a variety of classic Italian entrees perfect for any taste, and the location offers both dine-in and takeaway options. With its rich decorations and historical feel, it's a perfect spot for both casual dining and special occasions.

Accommodations

Banff International Hostel
Location: 449 Banff Ave, Banff, AB T1L 1A6, Canada
Contact: +1 403-985-7744
Website: www.banffinternationalhostel.com
Opening Hours:
- Check-in: 16:00
- Check-out: 11:00
Description: Banff International Hostel offers a practical and budget-friendly accommodation option in the heart of Banff National Park. Located just a 7-minute walk from the town center and 5 km from Banff Upper Hot Springs, this hostel is ideal for travelers looking to explore the local area and enjoy the natural beauty of the surrounding mountains and forests. The hostel provides a variety of amenities, including free parking, free breakfast, and complimentary Wi-Fi. The rooms, while basic, are designed to meet the needs of budget-conscious travelers, featuring large bathrooms and essential in-room facilities.

Brewster Mountain Lodge
Location: 208 Caribou St, Banff, AB T1L 1C1, Canada
Contact: +1 403-762-2900
Website: www.brewstermountainlodge.com
Opening Hours: Check-in time: 16:00, Check-out time: 11:00
Description: Brewster Mountain Lodge offers a charming, lodge-style accommodation experience in the heart of Banff. This hotel is conveniently located just a 2-minute walk from the Whyte Museum of the Canadian Rockies and 1.8 km from the Banff Centre for Arts and Creativity, making it an excellent base for exploring the cultural and natural attractions of the area. Guests can enjoy a range of amenities including free breakfast, excellent service, and a great location close to

downtown Banff's shopping, dining, and entertainment options. The hotel rooms are well-appointed, offering large, clean spaces with comfortable beds and beautiful views, though some guests note they could be updated.

Canalta Lodge
Location: 545 Banff Ave #1B5, Banff, AB T1L 1B5, Canada
Contact: +1 403-762-2112
Website: www.canaltalodge.com
Opening Hours: Check-in time: 16:00, Check-out time: 11:00
Description: Canalta Lodge is a 3-star hotel located within Banff National Park in the Rocky Mountains. This hotel offers a cozy yet refined setting ideal for guests looking to explore the natural beauty of Banff. Situated 4 km from the iconic Banff Springs Hotel and 7 km from the Banff Upper Hot Springs, it serves as a convenient base for visitors interested in outdoor activities and relaxation. The hotel features amenities including free Wi-Fi, complimentary breakfast, paid parking, wellness facilities, and luxurious room amenities. Rooms are well-equipped with modern comforts, providing a perfect blend of functionality and elegance. The property is easily accessible by car and is close to public transit, making it a strategic choice for tourists wanting to explore the local sights and shops.

Elk + Avenue Hotel
Location: 333 Banff Ave, Banff, AB T1L 1B1, Canada
Contact: +1 877-442-2623
Website: www.banffjaspercollection.com
Opening Hours: Check-in time: 16:00, Check-out time: 11:00
Description: The Elk + Avenue Hotel offers a vibrant, contemporary atmosphere right at the edge of Banff's bustling town center. This prime location within Banff National Park is ideal for visitors looking to explore the area's natural and cultural attractions, being just 2 km from the Trans-Canada Highway, 4 km from the Banff Gondola, and 8 km from Mount Norquay ski resort. The hotel offers modern accommodations and facilities including a restaurant, cafe, free Wi-Fi, and paid parking. Additional amenities such as accessible rooms and air conditioning ensure a comfortable stay for all guests. The hotel also includes Farm & Fire restaurant and Good Earth Coffeehouse right on the premises, providing convenient dining options for guests.

Fairmont Banff Springs
Location: 405 Spray Ave, Banff, AB T1L 1J4, Canada
Contact: +1 403-762-2211
Website: www.fairmont.com
Opening Hours: Check-in time: 16:00, Check-out time: 12:00
Description: The Fairmont Banff Springs, a stunning hotel styled like a castle, is located within Banff National Park, close to local landmarks such as Bow Falls and the Whyte Museum of the Canadian Rockies. This luxurious establishment offers a full-service spa, multiple dining options including the WALDHAUS Restaurant and the Rundle Bar, and extensive wellness facilities. The hotel is renowned for its splendid architecture and offers activities for all seasons, including a golf course and ski facilities. Amenities include both indoor and outdoor pools, a variety of shops, electric vehicle charging stations, and meeting and banquet facilities. This location serves as a full-featured resort, combining historical elegance with modern comforts and services.

HI Banff Alpine Centre
Location: 801 Hidden Ridge Way, Banff, AB T1L 1B3, Canada
Contact: +1 403-762-4123
Website: www.hihostels.ca
Opening Hours: Check-in time: 15:00, Check-out time: 11:00
Description: The HI Banff Alpine Centre offers a unique lodging experience in Banff National Park, located 6 km from the Banff Upper Hot Springs and 6.3 km from the scenic Banff Gondola rides up Sulphur Mountain. This hostel combines the charm of a lodge setting with the affordability and community vibe of hostel accommodation. It features both private and shared rooms, catering to diverse traveler needs, from solo adventurers to groups. Amenities include free Wi-Fi, a business center, and a café-bar on site that serves meals and drinks. The hostel also provides practical facilities such as a shared kitchen, laundry services, and free parking, making it an ideal base for exploring the natural beauty of Banff.

LAKE LOUISE

Lake Louise, located in the scenic Improvement District No. 9 within Banff National Park, is a breathtaking glacier-fed lake renowned for its vibrant turquoise waters. Surrounded by majestic mountain peaks and lush forests, Lake Louise offers visitors a captivating natural landscape to explore. Whether admiring the serene beauty of the lake from its shores or embarking on one of the many hiking trails that meander through the surrounding wilderness, visitors to Lake Louise are sure to be enchanted by its pristine beauty.

In addition to its stunning natural scenery, Lake Louise offers a range of recreational activities for outdoor enthusiasts. From leisurely walks along the lakeshore to more challenging hikes up nearby peaks, there's something for everyone to enjoy. During the summer months, visitors can rent canoes to paddle across the crystal-clear waters of the lake or take guided boat tours to learn about the area's history and ecology. For those visiting in the winter, Lake Louise transforms into a winter wonderland, offering opportunities for ice skating, snowshoeing, and cross-country skiing. The surrounding mountains also provide excellent terrain for downhill skiing and snowboarding, making Lake Louise a premier destination for winter sports enthusiasts.

Nearby attractions include the Lake Louise Ski Resort, known for its world-class skiing and snowboarding facilities, and the Fairmont Chateau Lake Louise, a historic luxury hotel offering stunning views of the lake and surrounding mountains. With its unparalleled natural beauty and wealth of recreational opportunities, Lake Louise is a must-visit destination for travelers seeking an unforgettable outdoor adventure in the Canadian Rockies.

Lake Louise Visitor Centre
Telephone: +1-403-522-3833
Email: ll.info@pc.gc.ca

ATTRACTIONS WITHIN THE VILLAGE OF LAKE LOUISE

Lake Louise Visitor Centre
Location: Samson Mall, 201 Village Rd, Lake Louise, AB T0L 1E0, Canada
Contact: +1 403-762-8421
Website: www.bannflakelouise.com
Opening Hours:
- Monday to Sunday: 9:00 AM – 5:00 PM

Description: The Lake Louise Visitor Centre serves as a gateway to exploring the breathtaking landscapes of Banff National Park. Situated in Samson Mall, this center provides invaluable information and assistance to visitors planning their adventures in the area. The knowledgeable and friendly staff offer guidance and suggestions for hiking, biking, camping, and kayaking, ensuring visitors make the most of their time in this stunning natural environment. The center also provides free Wi-Fi, a scarce amenity in the area, allowing visitors to stay connected while enjoying the wilderness.

Upon arrival, guests are greeted by modern and clean facilities, including restrooms conveniently located near the entrance. Inside, the spacious lobby houses an extensive information center and a customer service counter where visitors can obtain maps, brochures, and valuable insights into the area's attractions and activities. For those seeking souvenirs or gifts, a small gift shop is available, offering unique items to commemorate your visit to Lake Louise. Additionally, a small 3D relief map of Banff adds to the informative experience provided by the center.

Moraine Lake

Location: Improvement District No. 9, AB, Canada
Opening Hours:
- Open from June to October
- Shuttle required for access

Description:
Moraine Lake, located in Banff National Park, is celebrated for its striking blue-green waters, which are fed by glacier melt from above. The lake is encircled by the impressive peaks of the Valley of the Ten Peaks, providing a dramatic setting for various outdoor activities. Visitors can embark on the Rockpile Trail, a short hike that offers panoramic views of the lake and its alpine surroundings. Additionally, canoe rentals are

available, allowing for an engaging experience on the water with views from a different vantage point.

Planning is crucial when visiting Moraine Lake, especially during peak times, as access is controlled and primarily available through a shuttle service. Visitors are encouraged to book the shuttle well in advance to secure a spot. The lake's surroundings, including numerous hiking trails and scenic viewpoints, make it a popular destination for nature lovers and outdoor enthusiasts seeking to explore the natural beauty of Banff National Park.

Lake Agnes

Location: Improvement District No. 9, AB, Canada

Description: Lake Agnes, positioned high in the terrain of Banff National Park, offers visitors a unique blend of natural beauty and historical charm.
Known for its stunning emerald waters and the iconic Lake Agnes Tea House, the lake is accessible via a moderately challenging uphill hike from Lake Louise. The trail spans approximately 3.4 kilometers each way and is famed for its breathtaking vistas that include vibrant waterfalls, dense forests, and panoramic mountain views.

The Lake Agnes Tea House, a quaint stopover at the hike's summit, provides refreshments and a chance to rest while enjoying the serene lake views. This trail, suitable for families and hikers of varying abilities, promises a rewarding experience with every step.

Peyto Lake

Location: Improvement District No. 9, AB, Canada

Description: Peyto Lake is a stunning glacier-fed lake located in the heart of Banff National Park, renowned for its vivid turquoise waters and breathtaking scenery. This high-altitude lake is easily accessible from the Icefields Parkway, making it a must-visit destination for travelers exploring the Canadian Rockies. The lake offers spectacular views from the Bow Pass and its upper viewpoint, providing an ideal backdrop for photography and nature appreciation. Visitors can reach the lake via a short, steep hike from the nearby parking lot, covering about 0.5 miles to the main viewing areas.

The path is paved but can be slippery in winter, so appropriate footwear and caution are advised. Peyto Lake offers a particularly enchanting view during the winter months. However, the trail to the lake is not maintained during this period, which introduces an element of challenge to the hike. The path may be obscured by snow, making it difficult to discern the correct route. Additionally, the trail includes numerous roots and wet areas, and you may encounter significant deadfall and obstructions along the route. There are also a few steep sections that can be slippery and treacherous. Carrying hiking poles is advisable for added stability and safety. Visitors should exercise caution due to the steep and potentially hazardous slopes during this season.

Morant's Curve
Location: 45 Highway 1A, Improvement District No. 9, AB T1L 1K2, Canada
Description: Morant's Curve is a picturesque scenic spot located along Highway 1A in Improvement District No. 9, Alberta, Canada. Renowned for its stunning views and iconic bend in the railway track, this spot offers a captivating vantage point for railway enthusiasts and nature lovers alike.

The curve, named after Nicholas Morant, a photographer for the Canadian Pacific Railway, provides an excellent opportunity to witness trains passing through against the backdrop of the majestic Canadian Rockies. Visitors often find themselves in awe of the breathtaking scenery and the serenity of the surrounding landscape. While Morant's Curve is especially popular for train spotting, it also serves as an idyllic location for photography enthusiasts seeking to capture the beauty of the Canadian wilderness. The bend in the track adds a dynamic element to photographs, creating memorable and visually striking compositions.

For those seeking a peaceful retreat into nature, Morant's Curve offers a tranquil escape, with the gentle sounds of the forest and the occasional rumble of passing trains. Visitors can take leisurely walks in the area, soaking in the panoramic views of the Bow Valley and the surrounding mountains.

Fairview Lookout

Location: Banff National Park, Lake Louise, Alberta, Canada

Description: Fairview Lookout offers a rewarding 2.3-kilometer out-and-back trail experience within the breathtaking landscape of Banff National Park. This moderately challenging route is a popular choice for hikers and runners, particularly during the peak season from June to September. The trail provides a great introduction to Lake Louise hiking, featuring moderate elevation gain and stunning views along the way.

While the trail is not overly strenuous, it does include some areas of moderate elevation gain and steep sections, making it suitable for those prepared for a bit of a challenge. The lookout itself offers outstanding panoramic views, making the effort well worth it. Although initially surrounded by trees, hikers can venture further past the lookout towards the shoreline for even more scenic vistas.

Visitors should note that during the spring and early summer, there may be lingering snow patches along the trail, so wearing appropriate hiking footwear is recommended. Additionally, the trail is exposed to avalanche hazard during the winter months, and it's not recommended to visit between mid-October and mid-June.

Parking can be limited during peak seasons, so visitors are advised to consider alternative transportation options such as taking the bus, which offers a more reliable option for accessing the trail. More information about transportation options can be found on the Parks Canada website.

Kingmik Dog Sled Tours

Location: 16430 Hwy 1A, Lake Louise, AB T0L 1E0, Canada
Contact: +1 855-482-4592
Website: www.kingmikdogsledtours.com
Opening Hours: Daily, 8 AM – 6 PM
Description: Experience the thrill of dog sledding amidst the breathtaking landscapes of Lake Louise, Alberta, with Kingmik Dog Sled Tours. Rated 4.9 stars with 215 reviews, this tour promises an unforgettable adventure for individuals and families alike.

Embark on a journey through snow-touched forests, led by a team of enthusiastic sled dogs eager to pull you through the pristine wilderness. The tour offers stunning views of the surrounding mountains and forests, creating a picturesque setting for your dog sledding adventure.

Led by knowledgeable guides, including Megan, who boasts years of experience in dog sledding, the tour provides insights into the history and practice of this traditional mode of transport. Megan's stories and expertise add depth to the experience, enhancing your understanding and appreciation of dog sledding.

During the tour, you'll have the opportunity to interact with the sled dogs, petting and feeding them as they eagerly await their journey. The mushers, or sled drivers, are friendly and welcoming, ensuring a safe and enjoyable experience for all participants.

Wild Water Adventures

Location: Sales Office Only, 111 Lake Louise Dr, Lake Louise, AB T0L 1E0, Canada

Contact: +1 403-522-2211 | **Website:** www.wildwater.com

Opening Hours: Monday to Friday: 9:00 AM – 4:00 PM, Saturday & Sunday: Closed

Description: Wild Water Adventures offers thrilling white water rafting experiences on the Kicking Horse River, providing adventurers with unforgettable memories in the heart of nature.

Located within the Fairmont Château Lake Louise on Floor 1, the sales office serves as the starting point for these exhilarating excursions. Although the office operates limited hours, staff are available to assist visitors in planning and booking their rafting trips, ensuring a seamless and enjoyable experience.

Guests embark on guided rafting tours led by professional and experienced staff who prioritize safety while delivering an exciting journey down the river. Whether it's navigating through thrilling rapids or enjoying the scenic beauty of the surrounding landscape, each trip promises excitement and adventure.

Reviews from satisfied guests highlight the exceptional service provided by the staff, who are attentive, friendly, and knowledgeable about the river and its surroundings.

Accommodations and Services:

Fairmont Château Lake Louise
Location: 111 Lake Louise Dr, Lake Louise, AB T0L 1E0, Canada
Contact: +1 403-522-3511
Website: www.fairmont.com
Check-in time: 16:00 **Check-out time:** 12:00
Description: Fairmont Château Lake Louise presents an unparalleled experience amidst the breathtaking scenery of Lake Louise in Alberta, Canada. This iconic hotel offers a luxurious retreat for travelers seeking tranquility and elegance in the midst of nature's splendor. Whether visiting for a romantic getaway, a family vacation, or a special celebration, guests are greeted by the warmth of the staff and the awe-inspiring views of the surrounding landscape.
The rooms at Fairmont Château Lake Louise are exquisitely designed, providing comfort and sophistication with plush amenities and spacious accommodations. Each room boasts a comfortable bed and a large bathroom, ensuring a relaxing stay for every guest.

HI Lake Louise Alpine Centre
Location: 203 Village Rd, Lake Louise, AB T0L 1E0, Canada
Contact: +1 403-522-2200
Website: www.hihostels.ca
Check-in time: 16:00 **Check-out time:** 11:00
Description: Situated amidst the stunning Canadian Rockies within Banff National Park, HI Lake Louise Alpine Centre offers a cozy retreat for travelers seeking adventure and natural beauty. Just 1.7 km from the railway station and 3.5 km from Lake Louise Ski Resort, this chalet-style hostel provides an ideal base for exploring the picturesque surroundings.
Guests can choose from a variety of accommodations, including private rooms with views and kitchenettes, ensuring a comfortable stay for individuals, families, or groups. While some guests have noted smaller bathrooms and dated rooms, the overall experience is complemented by the affordable rates and convenient location.
The hostel's amenities include free Wi-Fi, complimentary parking, and accessibility features, ensuring convenience and comfort for all guests. Additionally, the hostel's friendly staff receive high praise for their attentive service and welcoming hospitality.

JASPER

Located in Jasper National Park, Jasper is a town celebrated for its relaxed atmosphere and stunning natural surroundings. The landscape, characterized by rugged mountains and deep valleys, was shaped by the same geological processes that formed Banff and has been known and utilized by Indigenous peoples for thousands of years before European contact. It became a part of the fur trade in the early 19th century, serving as a trading area and route for trappers.

Jasper Forest Park was established in 1907, with its status as a national park solidified in 1930. Initially less developed than Banff, Jasper has retained a more rugged and wild character. The construction of the Jasper Park Lodge in 1922 and the extension of the Canadian National Railway to Jasper in 1924 boosted tourism, making it a popular destination for nature lovers and adventurers.

Jasper National Park of Canada spans over 13,000 square kilometers and is renowned for its wildlife and scenic vistas. Visitors can engage in various activities such as camping, hiking, and wildlife viewing. The park features breathtaking landscapes from towering mountains to pristine rivers, offering visitors an unparalleled experience of nature's beauty. Popular attractions within the park include Athabasca Falls and Maligne Canyon, both known for their stunning views and exploration opportunities.

Facilities within the park, such as restrooms and camping sites, ensure a comfortable experience for all visitors. Admission is included in the purchase of a Jasper Park Pass, which is available at park entrances and select information locations in Jasper. Additional attractions include the Jasper SkyTram, which provides panoramic views of the surrounding mountains, and Friends of Jasper National Park, which offers opportunities for conservation and education.

Contact Information for Jasper National Park:
- **Phone number:** 780-852-6176
- **Email address:** jasperinfo@pc.gc.ca
- **Website:** https://parks.canada.ca/pn-np/ab/jasper

Attractions within Jasper National Park

Athabasca Falls

Description: Athabasca Falls offers a stunning natural spectacle just off the main road between Jasper and Banff. Visitors can enjoy the sight of the powerful waterfall, which is easily accessible from the parking area. The top path offers an easy walk with plenty of photo opportunities, while the lower canyons provide a more challenging experience, especially in winter when the trail and stairs can be slippery. Proper footwear is recommended for safety. The falls are fed by the Athabasca River, originating from the Columbia Icefields, adding to its grandeur. The park staff maintains the area year-round, ensuring cleanliness and safety for all visitors. Admission to Athabasca Falls is free, making it an accessible attraction for all. Nearby attractions include Sunwapta Falls, another natural wonder worth exploring.

Lac Beauvert
Opening Hours:
- Monday & Tuesday: 9 AM – 6 PM
- Thursday: 9 AM – 6 PM
- Sunday: 9 AM – 6 PM
- Wednesday & Friday & Saturday: 9 AM – 7 PM

Description: Lac Beauvert is a scenic lake nestled within Jasper National Park, offering serene hiking trails and picturesque golf courses. Visitors can enjoy leisurely strolls along the well-maintained trails, surrounded by the beauty of nature. The clear waters of the lake provide a stunning backdrop for outdoor activities and wildlife sightings, with elks frequently spotted in the area. The lake is also part of a larger resort and golf course, adding to its charm and recreational opportunities. Whether taking a peaceful stroll or enjoying a round of golf, Lac Beauvert offers a tranquil escape into the heart of the Canadian Rockies. Admission to Lac Beauvert is free, making it an accessible attraction for all. Nearby attractions include the Valley of the Five Lakes Trail, offering breathtaking views of five pristine lakes, and Whistlers Peak Trailhead, providing access to stunning mountain vistas.

Maligne Canyon

Description: Maligne Canyon is a scenic limestone canyon located within Jasper National Park, offering breathtaking views of waterfalls and natural wonders. Spanning 50 meters in depth, the canyon features multiple bridges that provide stunning vantage points for visitors to admire the surrounding landscape. The canyon is open year-round, allowing visitors to experience its beauty in every season. In winter, frozen waterfalls create a magical atmosphere, perfect for ice walking tours that provide a unique perspective of the canyon's icy formations. During warmer months, the canyon offers picturesque hiking trails, suitable for visitors of all skill levels. Whether exploring the canyon's depths or admiring its beauty from above, Maligne Canyon promises an unforgettable outdoor experience. Nearby attractions include Maligne Lookout, offering panoramic views of the surrounding mountains, and Whistlers Peak Trailhead, providing access to scenic hiking trails. Admission to Maligne Canyon is free, making it an accessible destination for nature lovers and outdoor enthusiasts alike.

Mount Edith Cavell

Location: Improvement District No. 12, AB T0E 1E0, Canada

Description: Mount Edith Cavell offers visitors a picturesque mountain experience in Jasper, Alberta. This iconic peak features various hiking and climbing trails, allowing outdoor enthusiasts to explore its natural beauty. One of the highlights of Mount Edith Cavell is the distinctive Angel Glacier, which captivates visitors with its breathtaking views. The mountain's trails vary in difficulty, catering to both casual hikers and experienced climbers. The trail to the glacier offers stunning panoramic views and opportunities for photography. Visitors should note that some areas of the trails can be steep and slippery, requiring caution. Additionally, access to the mountain involves driving on winding roads, with limited parking available. Despite the challenges, Mount Edith Cavell is a must-visit destination along the Icefields Parkway, offering a memorable outdoor adventure in the Canadian Rockies.

Sunwapta Falls

Description: Sunwapta Falls is a serene hiking area located in Jasper, Alberta, offering a refreshing retreat into nature. This picturesque destination features a stunning waterfall and breathtaking views of the surrounding landscape. Visitors can enjoy a short, easy walk from the well-maintained parking lot to reach the falls, making it accessible to all skill levels. The falls cascade gracefully through the canyon, creating a tranquil atmosphere that invites relaxation and reflection. With plenty of parking available, Sunwapta Falls is a convenient stop for travelers exploring the beauty of Jasper National Park. Whether you're seeking a peaceful stroll or simply want to admire the natural beauty of the area, Sunwapta Falls is sure to leave a lasting impression.

Valley of the Five Lakes
Description: The Valley of the Five Lakes offers a captivating hiking experience amidst the stunning landscapes of Jasper National Park. This picturesque trail features a series of five beautiful lakes, each with its own unique charm and color palette. The trail is well-maintained and suitable for hikers of all skill levels, offering both shorter and longer loop options. Along the way, visitors can immerse themselves in the natural beauty of

the Canadian Rockies, surrounded by lush forests, rolling hills, and breathtaking scenery. Wildlife sightings are common, with opportunities to encounter elk and other native species. Whether you're seeking a leisurely stroll or a more challenging hike, the Valley of the Five Lakes promises an unforgettable outdoor adventure. With ample parking available, it's easy to access this scenic trail and explore the wonders of Jasper's wilderness.

Miette Hot Springs

Location: Miette Rd Jasper, Miette Hotsprings, AB T0E 1E0, Canada
Contact: +1 800-767-1611
Website: www.hotsprings.ca
Monday to Sunday: 10:30 AM – 9:00 PM
Description: Nestled amidst the natural splendor of Jasper, Miette Hot Springs beckons visitors to indulge in relaxation and rejuvenation. Reopening each year in early May, this tranquil oasis offers al fresco pools filled with soothing spring water sourced from the surrounding mountains, boasting a comforting temperature of 104°F. As you soak in the therapeutic waters, you'll be treated to awe-inspiring scenic views, providing a serene backdrop for your experience. The facility also features a small restaurant serving delectable fare, perfect for refueling after your soak. Whether you're seeking relaxation, relief from muscle tension, or simply a moment of tranquility in nature, Miette Hot Springs promises a memorable and revitalizing visit. Advanced reservations are not required, but it's advisable to arrive early, especially during peak times, to secure your spot in this idyllic retreat.

Sulphur Skyline Trail
Description: The Sulphur Skyline Trail offers a challenging yet rewarding hiking experience within Jasper National Park. Spanning 7.9 kilometers as an out-and-back route, the trail features an elevation gain of 656 meters, providing hikers with stunning panoramic views. Known for its popularity among hikers,

snowshoers, and runners, the trail is best explored from June through October. Dogs are welcome but must remain on a leash.
The hike begins with a gradual uphill ascent, offering limited views until reaching a point where the trail emerges, revealing expansive vistas across the valleys. As hikers ascend, the trail becomes steeper, with numerous switchbacks leading to viewpoints overlooking the Fiddle Valley. Upon reaching the treeline, the terrain becomes more challenging, culminating in a final push to the summit.
While the trail may be difficult to follow in certain seasons due to snow accumulation, the panoramic views from the summit make the journey worthwhile. Utopia Mountain dominates the skyline, providing breathtaking views of the surrounding landscape. Descending the trail can be slippery, particularly in wet or snowy conditions, but hikers can enjoy a quick and easy descent.
At the trailhead's base, visitors can relax and unwind in the nearby hot springs, providing a perfect way to conclude the hike.

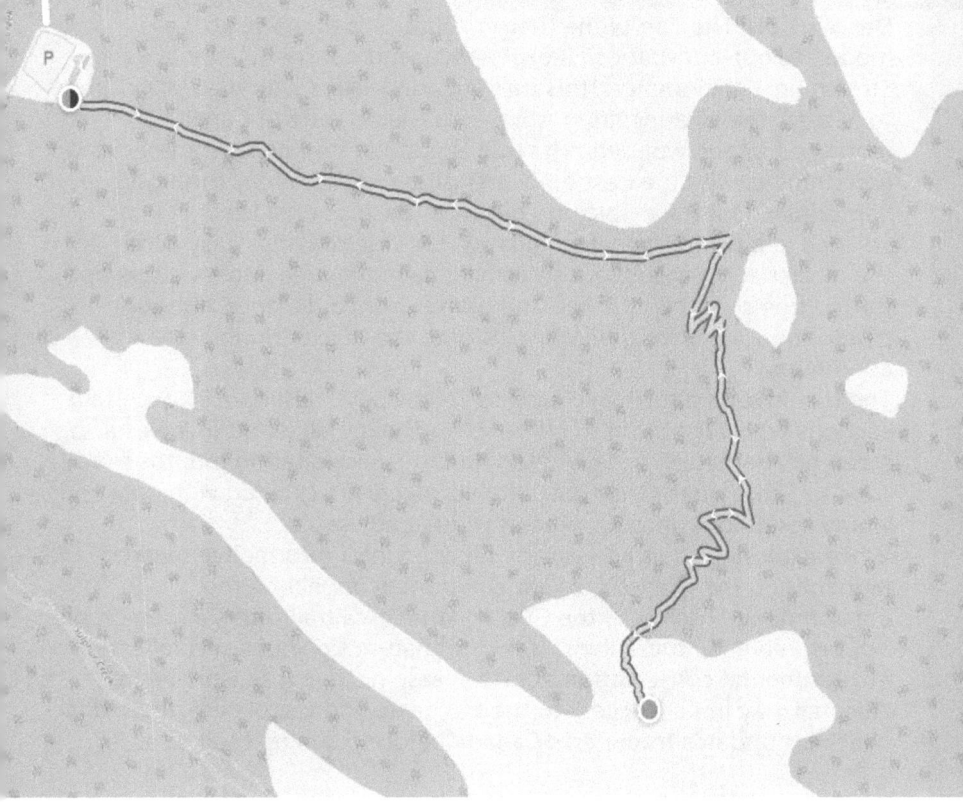

Toe of the Athabasca Glacier Trailhead

Description: The Toe of the Glacier Athabasca offers visitors a moderate out-and-back trail experience within Jasper National Park. Stretching 1.4 kilometers, this trail provides hikers with the opportunity to witness the awe-inspiring Athabasca Glacier, one of Canada's renowned frozen wonders. The trail is popular for hiking, snowshoeing, and running, with the best times to visit being from May through September. Dogs are welcome but must be kept on a leash.

Located just off the Icefields Parkway, the trail provides easy access to the glacier and various tourist attractions in the area. Most visitors opt for the free short hike to view the glacier from a distance, although paid options exist for guided walks onto the glacier during safe conditions.

The trail follows a relatively easy-to-follow path, albeit rocky in certain sections with large stones and pebbles. The initial ascent involves a steep hill, particularly challenging during peak visitation months from June to September. Once past the hill, hikers are greeted with cool and windy conditions, making protective gear advisable.

While exploring the trail, visitors will encounter informative markers highlighting the glacier's retreat and human impact on the environment. The Toe of the Glacier Athabasca trail offers a memorable opportunity to witness the splendor of nature's glaciers and reflect on environmental conservation efforts. Please note that seasonal road closures may impact access to the trailhead, and visitors are advised to check for updates from Parks Canada before planning their visit.

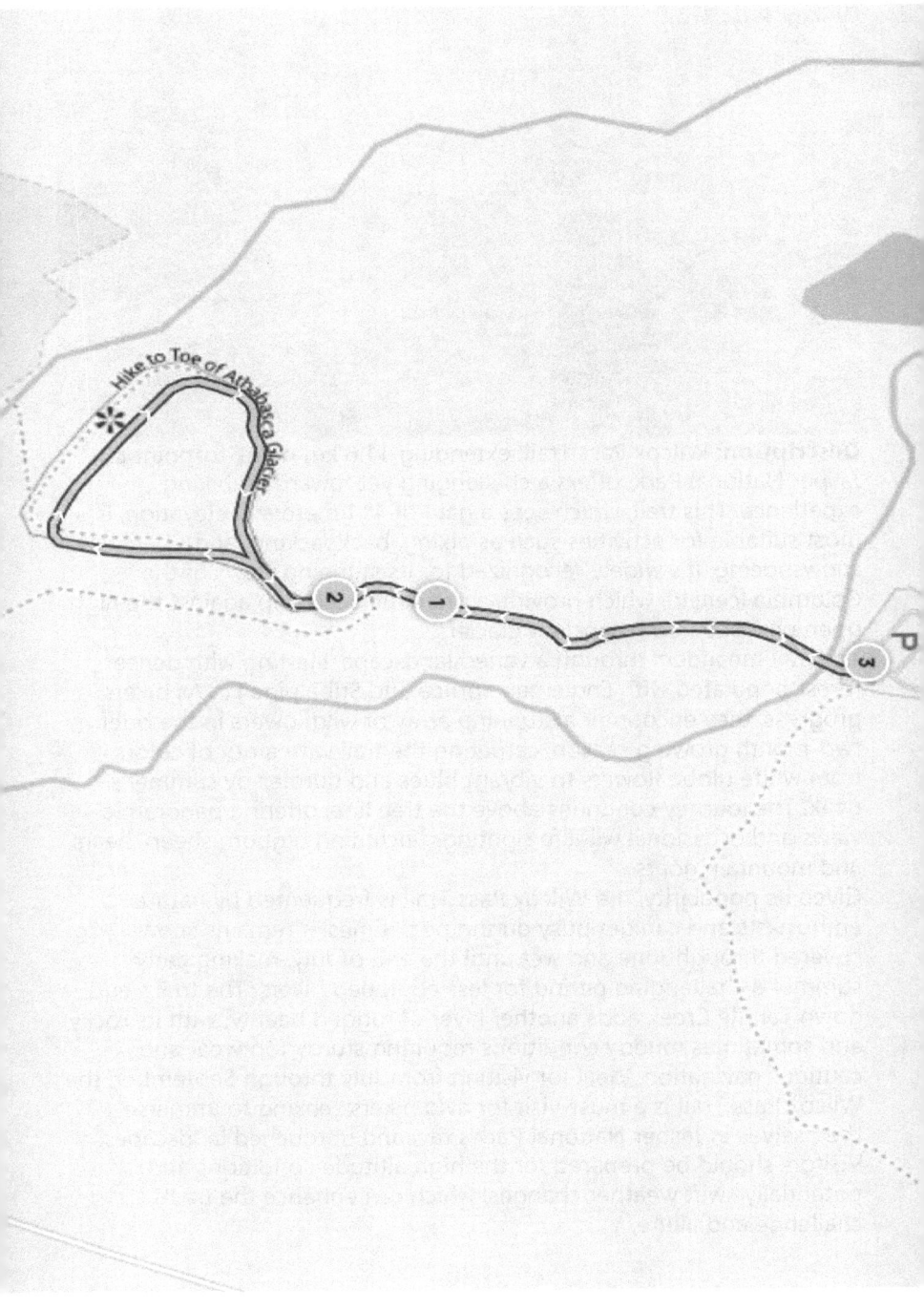

Wilcox Pass Trail

Description: Wilcox Pass Trail, extending 11.6 km point-to-point in Jasper National Park, offers a challenging yet rewarding hiking experience. This trail, which sees a gain of 411 meters in elevation, is most suitable for activities such as hiking, backpacking, and snowshoeing. It's widely recognized for its stunning views of the Columbia Icefield, which provide a dramatic backdrop against the high, open pass scoured by ancient glaciers.

The trail meanders through a varied landscape, starting with dense forest populated with Engleman Spruce and Subalpine Fir. As hikers progress, they encounter a stunning array of wildflowers in the brief two-month growing season, carpeting the trail with a riot of colors from white globe flowers to vibrant blues and purples by summer's peak. The journey continues above the tree line, offering panoramic views and occasional wildlife sightings, including bighorn sheep, bears, and mountain goats.

Given its popularity, the Wilcox Pass Trail is frequented by nature enthusiasts and can get busy during peak times. It remains snow-covered through June and wet until the end of July, making early summer a challenging period for less equipped hikers. The trail's end down Tangle Creek adds another layer of rugged beauty, with its rocky and sometimes muddy conditions requiring sturdy footwear and cautious navigation. Ideal for visiting from July through September, the Wilcox Pass Trail is a must-visit for avid hikers seeking to immerse themselves in Jasper National Park's raw and untouched landscapes. Visitors should be prepared for the high altitude conditions and potentially swift weather changes, which can enhance the trail's challenge and allure.

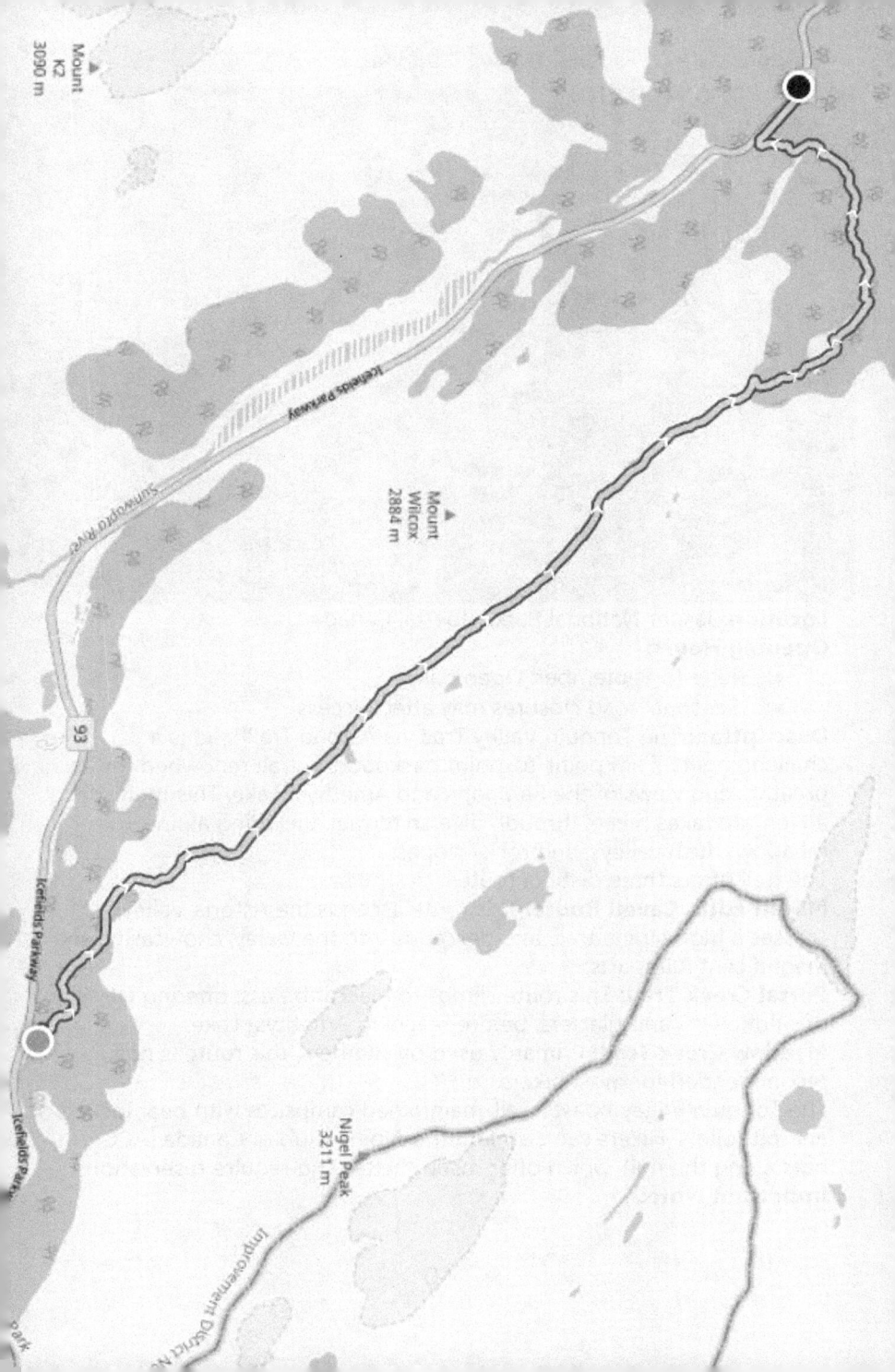

Tonquin Valley Trail via Astoria Trailhead

Location: Jasper National Park, Alberta, Canada
Opening Hours:
- June to September: Open daily
- Seasonal road closures may affect access

Description: The Tonquin Valley Trail via Astoria Trailhead is a challenging 41.7 km point-to-point backpacking trail renowned for its breathtaking views of the Ramparts and Amethyst Lake. This multi-day adventure takes hikers through diverse terrain, including alpine meadows, lush valleys, and rocky slopes.

The trail offers three distinct routes:

Mount Edith Cavell Route: This route ascends the Astoria Valley, crosses a high alpine trail, and descends into the valley, showcasing the magnificent Ramparts.

Portal Creek Trail: This route climbs to Maccarib Pass, offering views of wildflowers and glaciers, before reaching Amethyst Lake.

Meadow Creek Trail: Primarily used by climbers, this route is not recommended for most hikers.

The Tonquin Valley boasts well-maintained campsites with bear lockers and pit toilets. Hikers can also find the Alpine Club of Canada (ACC) huts along the trail, which offer rustic shelter and require reservations.

Important Note:

- Bring appropriate gear for backpacking and diverse weather conditions, including waterproof boots, trekking poles, and bug spray.
- Be prepared for mud, wet sections, and river crossings.
- As of September 2023, some bridges are out and require river crossings. Such as the route between the warden station and switchbacks on the Astoria approach, as it is decommissioned.
- Plan and book campsites in advance, as this is a popular trail.
- Be aware of potential wildlife encounters, including bears and caribou.
- Cell service is limited to the Portal trailhead.

Geraldine Lakes Trail: First Lake
Location: Jasper National Park, Alberta, Canada
Opening Hours:
- July to September: Open daily
- Seasonal road closures may affect access

Description: The Geraldine Lakes Trail to First Lake is a moderately challenging 5.1 km out-and-back hike within Jasper National Park. This trail winds through a lush forest, alongside a river, and features a stunning waterfall cascading into the first lake. The trail can be wet and muddy, especially near the lake, so waterproof hiking boots are recommended. While the hike to the first lake is considered moderate, continuing to the second lake involves challenging boulder hopping and steep scrambles. This trail is less frequented than other popular trails in the park, offering a more secluded experience. The best time to visit is during the summer months when the weather is warmer and drier.

Important Note:
- A high-clearance vehicle is recommended for accessing the trailhead due to rough road conditions.
- Bring bug spray, as mosquitoes can be prevalent, especially near the lake.
- Be prepared for muddy sections and wear appropriate footwear.
- If continuing past the first lake, be prepared for challenging boulder hopping and steep sections.
- While the trail is considered kid-friendly, the second lake portion is more suitable for experienced hikers.

Jasper SkyTram

Location: Whistlers Rd, Jasper, AB T0E 1E0, Canada
Contact: +1 780-852-3093
Website: www.jasperskytram.com
Hours: Monday to Sunday: 10:00 AM – 5:00 PM
Description: Jasper SkyTram offers an exhilarating aerial tram ride to a breathtaking viewpoint at an elevation of 2277 meters, providing visitors with panoramic vistas of the surrounding landscapes. The tram ride includes an onboard tour guide who enhances the experience with insightful commentary. Additionally, there is a hiking trail available for those who wish to explore further.

Situated on Whistlers Rd in Jasper, Alberta, the SkyTram operates daily from 10:00 AM to 5:00 PM, allowing ample time for visitors to enjoy the scenic ride and explore the summit. The tram provides swift transportation to the top, offering stunning views of Jasper and the surrounding mountains. Visitors can witness the majestic beauty of the area, with trees resembling matchsticks from the elevated vantage point.

Guests are encouraged to make reservations in advance, especially during peak times, to ensure a seamless experience. For those seeking adventure, snowshoes are available for rent or visitors can bring their own cleats for added traction on the trails, particularly during the ascent to the summit.

Marmot Basin

Location: 1 Marmot Rd, Jasper, AB T0E 1E0, Canada
Contact: +1 780-852-3816
Website: www.skimarmot.com
Description: Marmot Basin is a premier ski resort nestled in the stunning landscapes of Jasper, Alberta. Offering a diverse range of runs on varied terrains, Marmot Basin caters to skiers and snowboarders of all skill levels, from beginners to experts. With its easy access and ample parking, Marmot Basin provides a hassle-free experience for visitors.

The resort boasts excellent amenities, including chalets where guests can enjoy a selection of food and beverages. The Caribou Bar & Grill, located on the first floor, offers a variety of dishes, with highlights such as

tasty chili and filling meals. Additionally, the Smoke House mid-mountain is renowned for its great meats, providing a satisfying dining experience for guests seeking a break from the slopes.

Marmot Basin is praised for its breathtaking views and well-maintained trails. The Eagle East runs are particularly enjoyable, offering thrilling experiences, especially after a fresh dump of snow. Visitors can also take advantage of the reasonable prices for food and drinks at the chalets, making it a convenient and enjoyable destination for a day on the slopes.

While the resort is temporarily closed, it typically operates until the end of April, allowing ample time for winter sports enthusiasts to enjoy the snowy slopes.

Overall, Marmot Basin promises an unforgettable skiing or snowboarding experience amidst the natural beauty of Jasper National Park. Whether seeking adrenaline-pumping adventures or leisurely runs, Marmot Basin offers something for everyone, making it a must-visit destination for winter sports enthusiasts.

Maligne Lake
Location: Improvement District No. 12, AB, Canada
Opening Hours: • Open year-round, but access depends on seasonal conditions.
Description: Maligne Lake, nestled within Jasper National Park, is renowned for its stunning natural beauty and is one of the park's signature attractions. This scenic lake is about a 1-hour drive from Jasper townsite and is famous for its clear blue waters, Spirit Island, and the dramatic backdrop of surrounding mountains and glaciers. Visitors can enjoy a variety of activities at Maligne Lake, including the popular Maligne Lake Cruise that takes them to the iconic Spirit Island, offering spectacular views and photo opportunities. The lake is also a favorite spot for kayaking, canoeing, and fishing, with rentals available during the summer months. Hiking enthusiasts will find several trails around the lake, providing ample opportunities to explore the area's rich wildlife and scenic landscapes. The area is known for sightings of moose and bears, adding an element of adventure to every visit. During the winter, the lake transforms into a quiet, snowy wonderland, ideal for snowshoeing and cross-country skiing. Despite the lake's accessibility challenges during colder months, it remains a captivating destination for those willing to brave the cold. With its expansive parking lot, including space for RVs, and available toilet facilities, Maligne Lake is well-equipped to handle visitors. Whether seeking a serene paddle across the water, a vigorous hike, or a leisurely cruise, Maligne Lake offers an unforgettable experience in one of Canada's most picturesque settings.

Skyline Trail

Opening Hours: The trail is typically accessible from May through October, but conditions can vary.

Description: Renowned as one of the best backpacking trails in the Canadian Rockies, the Skyline Trail offers a challenging yet rewarding 44.9-km trek through Jasper National Park. Over half the trail is above the treeline, providing breathtaking alpine vistas of surrounding mountains, valleys, and lakes. While most hikers complete the trail in 2-3 days, experienced hikers can finish it in a single day (10-12 hours). The trail is well-maintained but can be muddy or snowy depending on the season. Campsite reservations are required and can be made through the Parks Canada website.

Hikers should be prepared for varied weather conditions, carry sufficient layers, and be aware of potential wildlife encounters. It is recommended to hike from south (Maligne Lake) to north (Maligne Canyon) to minimize elevation gain. The trailhead at Maligne Lake is a scenic one-hour drive from the town of Jasper.

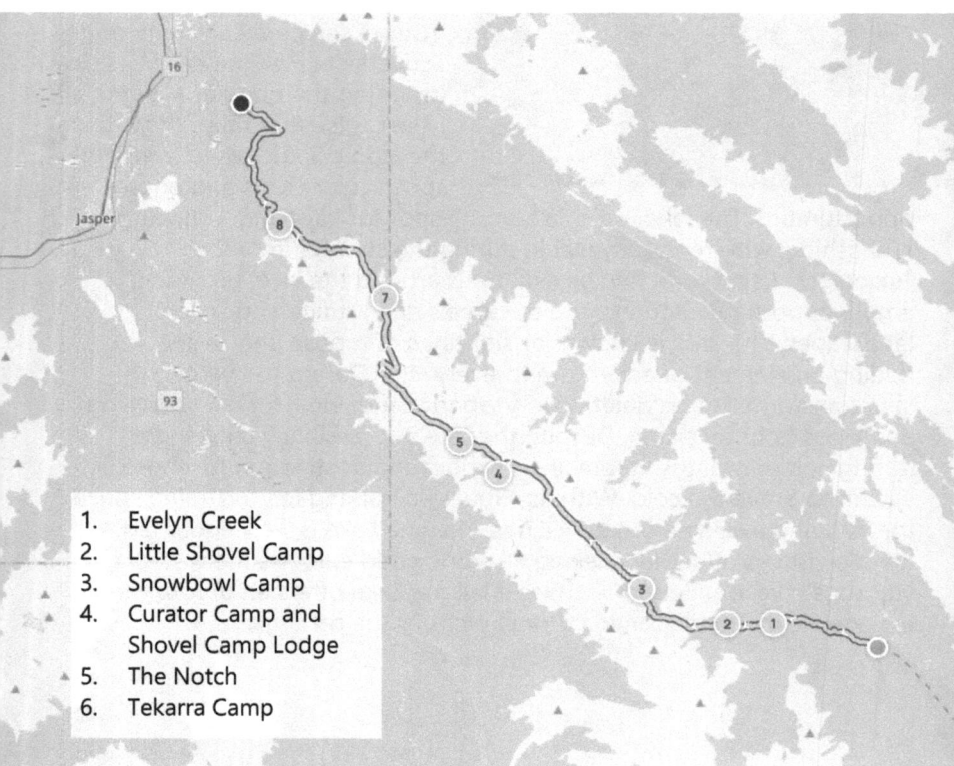

1. Evelyn Creek
2. Little Shovel Camp
3. Snowbowl Camp
4. Curator Camp and Shovel Camp Lodge
5. The Notch
6. Tekarra Camp

Whistlers Trail

Opening Hours: March to October: Open daily
- Seasonal road closures may affect access

Description: The Whistlers Trail is a challenging 16.6 km out-and-back hike offering a diverse range of terrain and spectacular views of Jasper National Park. Beginning with a gradual ascent through a forested area, the trail then leads hikers through a boulder field, where the peak becomes visible. The final section is the most demanding, with a steep incline through a light forest before reaching the summit. For those seeking a less strenuous experience, the Jasper SkyTram provides access to the upper portion of the trail. Hikers can take the tram up and complete the final 30-45 minute climb to the summit, or hike the entire trail and take the tram back down.

Due to its popularity, the trail and SkyTram station can get busy. The trail is also home to various wildlife, so hikers should be aware of their surroundings.

Important Note:
- Bring appropriate gear for the weather and terrain, including sturdy hiking boots, layers, sunscreen, a hat, and plenty of water.
- Be prepared for a challenging hike with significant elevation gain.
- As of June 2024, the trail is still experiencing significant snow cover, so hikers should be prepared for difficult conditions and consider using snowshoes.

Campgrounds and Outdoor Living within Jasper National Park

Wabasso Campground

Location: AB-93A, Jasper, AB T0E 1E0, Canada
Contact: +1 877-737-3783
Description: Wabasso Campground offers a tranquil retreat amidst the natural beauty of Jasper National Park. Situated along the riverfront, this campground provides a peaceful setting for campers seeking a quiet escape. With basic amenities including firewood and clean toilets, Wabasso Campground ensures a comfortable camping experience for visitors.

The spacious campsites accommodate various camping setups, from tents to RVs. While some areas lack shade due to tree removal, the campground offers ample space for relaxation and outdoor activities. Guests can enjoy gathering around the fire pit, with plenty of wood provided for campfires.

The campground's cleanliness is commendable, with immaculate restroom facilities maintained by diligent park staff. Some bathrooms even feature dishwashing stations outside for added convenience. Wabasso Campground prioritizes visitor comfort and satisfaction, with friendly staff available to assist guests as needed.

Campers at Wabasso Campground can revel in the tranquility of the surrounding nature, with the soothing sound of the rushing river adding to the serene atmosphere. Public restrooms are equipped with sinks for handwashing, ensuring hygienic facilities for campers' convenience.

Wapiti Campground
Location: RWVJ+GF, AB-93A, Jasper, AB T0E 1E0, Canada
Contact: +1 780-852-6176
Hours:
Check-in Time: 14:00
Check-out Time: 11:00
Description: Wapiti Campground offers a serene retreat amidst the natural beauty of Jasper National Park. Situated along the tranquil riverbanks, the campground provides a peaceful setting for camping enthusiasts. Both tent and RV campers are welcome, with spacious sites featuring picnic tables and fire pits. The campground boasts clean restroom facilities, including hot showers and dishwashing stations, ensuring a comfortable stay for visitors. Nature lovers will appreciate the picturesque river paths, perfect for leisurely strolls and wildlife sightings. Conveniently located near Jasper, Wapiti Campground provides easy access to town amenities while immersing guests in the wilderness.

Snaring Campground
Location: Snaring Rd, Jasper, AB T0E 1E0, Canada

Description: Located amidst the breathtaking natural beauty of Jasper National Park, Snaring Campground offers a serene escape for campers seeking tranquility and immersion in nature. This simple yet charming campground provides all the essential amenities for a comfortable stay, including firewood, toilet facilities, and potable water. The spacious campsites offer privacy and seclusion, allowing guests to enjoy the peaceful surroundings undisturbed. Situated within walking distance of the picturesque Snaring River, campers can indulge in leisurely strolls or simply relax by the water's edge, soaking in the stunning mountain views. While the campground does not feature showers or dishwashing areas, its rustic charm and striking natural setting make it a popular choice for nature lovers and outdoor enthusiasts alike. Whether you're seeking a quiet retreat or a basecamp for outdoor adventures, Snaring Campground provides the perfect setting to unwind and connect with the wilderness.

Honeymoon Lake Campground
Location: Hwy, 93 Icefields Pkwy, Jasper, AB T0E 1E0, Canada
Contact: +1 877-737-3783
Description: Located along the scenic Icefields Parkway in Jasper National Park, Honeymoon Lake Campground offers a serene escape amidst the majestic Canadian Rockies. This expansive campground, with 35 tent and RV pitches, provides a stunning backdrop of the tranquil lake and surrounding mountains, creating an idyllic setting for nature enthusiasts.

Guests can enjoy the beauty of lakeside camping while being surrounded by pristine wilderness. Essential amenities include fire pits for cozy evening gatherings and sanitary facilities for added convenience. Campers can relax and unwind in this peaceful environment, immersing themselves in the beauty of the crystal-clear lake and the lush forest scenery. With options for both tent and RV camping, Honeymoon Lake Campground caters to various preferences, welcoming solo travelers, families, and couples alike.

Jonas Creek Campground
Location: AB-93, Jasper, AB T0E 1E0, Canada
Contact: +1 877-737-3783
Website: www.parks.canada.ca
Description: Jonas Creek Campground offers a serene camping experience amidst the natural beauty of Jasper National Park. Situated along AB-93, the

campground provides easy access to the park's attractions. Campers can enjoy tent and motorhome sites, with RVs up to 25 feet in length welcome. The campground features picnic shelters, toilet facilities, and complimentary firewood. Please note that there are no shower facilities available on-site. Despite its proximity to the highway, the campground maintains a tranquil ambiance, with the soothing sounds of a nearby creek adding to its charm. Jonas Creek Campground is perfect for those seeking a simple and enjoyable camping retreat in the heart of Jasper National Park.

Wilcox Creek Campground
Location: Icefields Pkwy, Jasper, AB T0E 1E0, Canada
Contact: +1 877-737-3783
Website: www.pc.gc.ca
Opening Hours: Temporarily closed
Description: Wilcox Creek Campground offers a tranquil retreat in the heart of Jasper National Park. Nestled along Icefields Parkway, this secluded campground provides an escape into nature with picturesque views of the surrounding landscape. While temporarily closed, the campground typically features potable water, cooking shelters, and pit toilets for visitors' convenience. Camping spots range from those offering stunning views on campsites 1-7 to more private and secluded options with higher numbers. The campground is known for its well-maintained facilities, including numerous outhouses conveniently located near each site. Visitors are advised to park their vehicles cautiously to avoid the edge, as some areas have potential hazards. Despite its temporary closure, Wilcox Creek Campground remains a popular destination for outdoor enthusiasts seeking a peaceful camping experience amidst the natural beauty of Jasper National Park.

Columbia Icefield Campground
Location: Icefields Pkwy, Jasper, AB T0E 1E0, Canada
Time: Check-in: 14:00, Check-out: 11:00
Description: Columbia Icefield Campground offers a serene retreat amidst the natural beauty of Jasper National Park. Conveniently located off Icefields Parkway, this campground  provides easy access to the nearby glacier and stunning waterfall views. Although situated near the highway, visitors are pleasantly surprised by the lack of highway noise, allowing for a peaceful camping experience. The campground features a handful of spots with breathtaking views, while the majority offer a tranquil forested setting. Amenities include pit toilets and self-registration, with firewood and potable water available on-site. Due to its popularity, it operates on a first-come, first-served basis, making it essential to arrive early, particularly on weekends. With its scenic surroundings and convenient proximity to the Columbia Icefield Visitor Center, Columbia Icefield Campground is an ideal base for exploring the wonders of Jasper National Park.

Miette Campground

Location: Miette Rd, Improvement District No. 12, AB T0E 0E0, Canada
Check-out Time: 11:00
Description: Miette Campground offers a tranquil retreat nestled within the stunning landscapes of Improvement District No. 12. Situated amidst tall trees, this campground

provides ample privacy and shade for campers. The spacious layout features well-equipped campsites with fire pits and picnic tables, ensuring a comfortable camping experience. Clean and modern bathrooms with flush toilets are conveniently located throughout the campground, providing added convenience for visitors. Additionally, a covered eating area with a public sink adds to the amenities available on-site. One of the highlights of Miette Campground is the provision of free firewood, allowing guests to enjoy cozy campfires under the starlit skies. The campground staff are known for their friendly and helpful demeanor, contributing to the overall positive experience for visitors. While Miette Campground offers a serene atmosphere, it is also conveniently located near various recreational opportunities. Hiking trails, waterfalls, and scenic viewpoints are within easy reach, providing ample opportunities for outdoor exploration and adventure. However, it's essential to note that the campground's popularity can make booking a challenge, especially during peak seasons.

ATTRACTIONS WITHIN THE TOWN OF JASPER

Jasper-Yellowhead Museum & Archives

Location: 400 Bonhomme St, Jasper, AB T0E 1E0, Canada
Contact: +1 780-852-3013
Website: www.jaspermuseum.org
Opening Hours:
- Thursday to Sunday: 10 AM – 5 PM
- Closed on Monday to Wednesday

Description: Jasper-Yellowhead Museum & Archives offers a captivating journey through the history of Jasper and its surrounding region. Nestled in the heart of the town, this quaint museum showcases an array of artifacts, photographs, and displays that chronicle the area's rich heritage. From secret World War II

experiments on Lake Patricia to tales of fur trading and warden uniforms, visitors are treated to a diverse range of exhibits that illuminate the past.

The museum's collection also delves into the exploration of the area and the First Nations' history, providing valuable insights into the cultural tapestry of Jasper. Visitors can explore exhibits on notable figures such as Edith Cavell, further enriching their understanding of the region's significance.

While the museum may not be extensive in size, its exhibits are thoughtfully curated and offer a wealth of information for history enthusiasts and casual visitors alike. Entry is by donation, making it accessible to all. Additionally, visitors can browse through a selection of books for sale, including works about and by First Nations, adding to the educational offerings of the museum.

Two Brothers Totem Pole

Location: 416 Connaught Dr, Jasper, AB T0E 1E0, Canada

Description: The Two Brothers Totem Pole in Jasper, Alberta, is a historical landmark that stands as a significant cultural artifact. Carved by Jaalen and Gwaai Edenshaw, celebrated Haida artists, this totem pole was erected in 2011 and measures 13.7 meters in height. It is located off the main street in Jasper, making it an accessible stop for visitors exploring the area.

This totem pole symbolizes the connection between the Haida people of the west coast islands of Haida Gwaii and the Rocky Mountains. Its rich history and cultural significance are depicted through intricate carvings that narrate stories of journeys and relationships. The pole is strategically placed next to Jasper Railway Station, making it a striking feature for both residents and tourists.

Visitors can easily find street parking nearby and enjoy other attractions within walking distance. While exploring, take the opportunity to learn about the Aboriginal history and culture through the informative signs accompanying the totem pole.

Jasper Park Information Center

Location: 500 Connaught Dr, Jasper, AB T0E 1E0, Canada
Contact: +1 780-820-1006
Website: www.jasper.travel.com
Hours: Monday to Sunday: 9 AM – 5 PM

Description: The Jasper Park Information Center serves as a vital hub for visitors to Jasper National Park, offering valuable resources, maps, and travel tips. Situated conveniently on Connaught Drive, this visitor center provides essential information for exploring the park's natural wonders. In addition to its informational services, the center features a gift shop where visitors can purchase souvenirs to commemorate their visit. Whether you're seeking advice on hiking trails, wildlife viewing, or scenic drives, the knowledgeable staff at the Jasper Park Information Center are ready to assist. With its prime location and wealth of resources, this center is an indispensable resource for making the most of your Jasper adventure.

Mountain Galleries

Location: 1 Old Lodge Rd, Jasper, AB T0E 1E0, Canada
Contact: +1 780-852-5378
Website: www.mountaingalleries.com

Description: Mountain Galleries is an art lover's haven nestled within the Fairmont Jasper Park Lodge. This exquisite gallery showcases a diverse collection of paintings and sculptures, including works by Canadian artists. Visitors can immerse themselves in the beauty of local landscapes depicted in stunning artwork, capturing the essence of Jasper National Park and its surroundings. Whether you're an art enthusiast or simply appreciate fine craftsmanship, a visit to Mountain Galleries promises a memorable experience. Take a leisurely stroll through the gallery's elegant space, admiring the talent and creativity on display.

Jasper Art Gallery

Location: 500 Robson St, Jasper, AB T0E 1E0, Canada
Contact: +1 780-852-1994 | **Website:** www.jasperartistsguild.com
Hours: Thursday to Saturday: 10 AM – 6 PM | Closed Sunday to Wednesday
Description: Jasper Art Gallery is a charming haven for art enthusiasts, nestled away on Robson Street in Jasper. Featuring a diverse array of artwork by local artists, this gallery offers a unique opportunity to immerse yourself in the creative spirit of the community. From paintings to sculptures, visitors can explore a variety of mediums and styles, each reflecting the beauty and character of the surrounding landscape. The friendly staff are eager to share their knowledge and passion for art, making every visit a delightful experience. Whether you're seeking a new addition to your collection or simply wish to appreciate the talent of local artisans, Jasper Art Gallery welcomes you to discover the vibrant art scene thriving in the heart of Jasper.

Tour Services and Adventure Activities

Jasper Motorcycle Tours
Location: 610 Patricia St, Jasper, AB T0E 1E0, Canada
Contact: +1 780-931-6100
Website: www.jaspermotorcycletours.com
Description: Jasper Motorcycle Tours offers an exhilarating way to explore the stunning landscapes of Jasper and its surrounding areas. With a fleet of well-maintained motorcycles and experienced guides, adventurers can embark on thrilling journeys through rugged

mountain terrain and scenic highways. Whether you're a seasoned rider or a novice, the tours cater to all levels of experience, ensuring a safe and enjoyable adventure for everyone. Feel the rush of the open road as you wind through majestic mountain passes and witness breathtaking vistas at every turn. The friendly and knowledgeable staff provide personalized service, sharing their passion for motorcycling and local knowledge along the way. From half-day excursions to full-day adventures, Jasper Motorcycle Tours offers unforgettable experiences that showcase the natural beauty of the Canadian Rockies from a unique perspective.

Jasper Food Tours
Location: 500 Connaught Dr, Jasper, AB T0E 1E0, Canada
Contact: +1 780-931-3287
Website: www.jasperfoodtours.com
Opening Hours: Daily: 9 AM – 9 PM
Description: Indulge in a culinary adventure through the heart of Jasper with Jasper Food Tours. Offering a variety of curated experiences, including the Downtown Foodie Tour, Peak-Nic, and Bites on E-Bikes, this tour agency provides a delicious exploration of Jasper's vibrant food scene. Led by knowledgeable guides, visitors have the opportunity to sample delectable dishes and drinks from four different restaurants while learning about the area's culture and history. Whether you're a food enthusiast, a history buff, or simply looking for a unique way to experience Jasper, Jasper Food Tours promises an unforgettable journey filled with great food, drinks, and camaraderie. With a perfect rating from satisfied customers, this tour agency is a must-visit for anyone craving a taste of Jasper's culinary delights.

Maligne Lake Cruise
Location: Maligne Lake Rd, Improvement District No. 12, AB T0E 1E0, Canada
Contact: +1 866-606-6700
Website: www.banffjaspercollection.com
Hours: Monday to Sunday: 9 AM – 5:30 PM
Description: The Maligne Lake Cruise offers a serene journey through the stunning landscapes of Maligne Lake in Jasper, Alberta. Visitors can embark on a 1.5-hour

cruise guided by knowledgeable tour guides, providing insights into the area's rich history and natural wonders. The cruise includes highlights such as Spirit Island, a picturesque spot perfect for capturing breathtaking photos of the surrounding mountains and glaciers. Reservations are recommended for this popular attraction, ensuring a smooth and enjoyable experience for all passengers. The cruise operates year-round, allowing visitors to marvel at the beauty of Maligne Lake in every season. Amenities onboard include restaurants, washroom facilities, and comfortable seating, ensuring a pleasant journey for passengers of all ages. Nearby attractions include Maligne Adventures offering a variety of outdoor excursions, and Maligne

Jasper Planetarium & Dark Sky Telescope Tours

Location: INSIDE the Fairmont hotel lobby, 1 Old Lodge Rd, Jasper, AB T0E 1E0, Canada
Contact: +1 780-931-3275 | **Website:** www.jasperplanetarium.com
Opening Hours: Monday: Closed | Tuesday to Sunday: 4 PM – 11:30 PM
Description: Located within the Fairmont Jasper Park Lodge, The Jasper Planetarium & Dark Sky Telescope Tours offer an extraordinary celestial experience. Delve into the wonders of the universe with expert guides, starting with a captivating planetarium show. Learn about constellations, planets, and the mesmerizing Northern Lights. Following the indoor presentation, step outside to explore the night sky through powerful telescopes. Witness planets, star clusters, and even galaxies, all while gaining insightful commentary from knowledgeable astronomers. Despite occasional cloud cover, guests receive a rain check valid for two years, ensuring they can return for another chance to marvel at the cosmos.

Rockaboo Mountain Adventures
Location: 610 Patricia St, Jasper, AB T0E 1E0, Canada
Contact: +1 780-820-0092
Website: www.rockaboo.ca
Hours: Monday to Sunday: 9 AM – 4:30 PM
Description: Rockaboo Mountain Adventures offers thrilling outdoor experiences amidst Jasper's stunning natural landscapes. Choose from a variety of exhilarating activities, including rock climbing, glacier hikes, and ice climbing, all led by experienced guides who prioritize safety and education. Embark on a journey to conquer the region's majestic peaks, whether scaling sheer rock faces or traversing icy glaciers. The small group sizes ensure personalized attention and instruction, making it accessible for both beginners and experienced adventurers alike. With each excursion, participants gain new skills, confidence, and unforgettable memories in the heart of the Canadian Rockies. Explore the wilderness with Rockaboo Mountain Adventures and discover the awe-inspiring beauty of Jasper National Park.

Canadian Skyline Adventures
Location: Jasper, AB, Canada
Contact: +1 780-883-0465
Website: www.canadianskylineadventures.com
Description: Canadian Skyline Adventures offers unforgettable outdoor experiences in the breathtaking landscapes of Jasper. Whether you're an experienced hiker or a novice adventurer, their knowledgeable guides provide safe and enjoyable excursions tailored to your preferences. From day hikes to multi-day backpacking trips, each journey is infused with stunning scenery and opportunities to encounter wildlife. Explore iconic peaks like Opal Peak and Bald Hills, or venture off the beaten path to discover hidden gems like Jacques Lake. With a focus on safety, education, and environmental stewardship, Canadian Skyline Adventures ensures every participant has a memorable and enriching experience in the heart of the Canadian Rockies.

Jasper Hikes and Tours Inc.
Location: 1004 Patricia St #6, Jasper, AB T0E 1E0, Canada
Contact: +1 780-931-4453 | **Website:** www.jasperhikesandtours.ca
Opening Hours: Monday to Sunday: 8 am – 8 pm
Description: Jasper Hikes and Tours Inc. offers thrilling outdoor adventures amidst the stunning landscapes of Jasper. With a team of experienced guides, they provide a range of hiking and tour options suitable for all levels of adventurers. Explore the wonders of Maligne Canyon on an exhilarating IceWalk, or embark on a half-day or full-day hike to immerse yourself in the natural beauty of the region. Each excursion is led by knowledgeable guides who prioritize safety and ensure a memorable experience for every participant. Whether you're seeking a leisurely stroll or a challenging trek, Jasper Hikes and Tours Inc. has something for everyone. With personalized attention and expert guidance, you'll discover the hidden gems of Jasper's wilderness and create unforgettable memories along the way.

Jasper Rafting Adventures

Location: 618C Connaught Dr, Jasper, AB T0E 1E0, Canada
Contact Information: +1 780-852-4292
Website: www.jasperraftingadventures.com
Hours: • Wednesday to Sunday: 10 AM – 6 PM
• Closed on Mondays and Tuesdays
Description: Jasper Rafting Adventures provides thrilling white-water rafting experiences on rivers such as the Athabasca and Sunwapta. Key offerings include the Athabasca River Mile 5, a family-friendly ride through class 2 rapids, and the more intense Athabasca Falls Run. Prices for these experiences convert to approximately $87 for the Mile 5 and $104 for the Falls Run. Advanced bookings are recommended, especially during peak seasons, to secure a spot.

Jasper Riding Stables

Location: 4km North on Pyramid Lake Rd, Jasper, AB T0E 1E0, Canada
Contact Information: +1 780-852-7433
Website: www.jasperstables.com
Hours: • Tuesday to Monday: 9 AM – 5 PM

Description: Jasper Riding Stables offers a range of horseback riding experiences through the picturesque landscapes of Jasper National Park. The stable provides guided tours that are suitable for both beginners and experienced riders. Rides traverse diverse terrains featuring stunning vistas, beautiful lakes, and shaded areas with aspen trees, enhancing the outdoor adventure. Advanced booking is recommended to secure a spot, especially during peak tourist seasons. The stable is conveniently located near other attractions such as Jasper SkyTram and Patricia Lake, making it an ideal addition to any visit to the park.

Pure Outdoors

Location: 632 Connaught Dr, Jasper, AB T0E 1E0, Canada
Contact Information: +1 780-852-4717
Website: www.pureoutdoors.ca
Opening Hours: • Tuesday to Monday: 10 AM – 6 PM • Saturday: 10 AM – 7 PM

Description: Pure Outdoors, formerly known as Skis Please, has served the Jasper community for over 25 years, evolving from a winter-focused equipment rental to a year-round adventure outfitter. Located strategically in Jasper National Park, Pure Outdoors offers a wide range of rental equipment suitable for both summer and winter activities, ensuring visitors are well-equipped for the region's diverse outdoor experiences.

From kayaking on Maligne Lake to snowshoeing through picturesque trails, Pure Outdoors provides quality gear for all skill levels. The shop offers convenient rental terms, including consecutive multi-day rental discounts, and custom rental experiences tailored to specific adventure needs. The staff, known for their local expertise and friendly service, also offer valuable advice and recommendations for exploring the natural beauty of Jasper.

For those seeking water adventures, Pure Outdoors specializes in custom experiences on the Athabasca River and surrounding waters, providing everything from relaxed day trips to thrilling multi-day expeditions.

Maligne Lake Boat House
Location: Maligne Lake Rd, Improvement District No. 12, AB T0E 1E0, Canada
Contact Information: +1 888-900-6272
Website: www.banffjaspercollection.com
Opening Hours: • Tuesday to Monday: 10 AM – 5 PM
Description: Maligne Lake Boat House offers a range of watercraft rentals, including canoes, single and tandem kayaks, and pedal boats, providing visitors with the opportunity to explore the serene Maligne Lake. Located 48 km from downtown Jasper, this boat house, originally built by the famed local explorer Donald "Curly" Phillips, is the starting point for a quintessential Canadian Rockies adventure.

Visitors can rent equipment by the hour or for a full day, with prices starting from $65 for a single kayak and up to $160 for a full-day canoe rental. Safety is a priority, and all equipment users must be at least eighteen years old or have a waiver signed by a parent. Children under 16 must be accompanied by a guardian. Due to the popularity of this destination and limited equipment availability, booking online in advance is recommended to guarantee your rental, although some equipment is available on a first-come, first-served basis on-site.

The Maligne Lake Boat House operates seasonally, allowing guests to paddle through crystal-clear waters and enjoy breathtaking views of surrounding mountainous terrain and potentially spot wildlife such as moose and black bears. Despite its remote location and the potential for crowded conditions, the unique experience of navigating one of Jasper's most beautiful lakes makes it well worth the visit.

Accommodations and Dining

Alpine Village Jasper
Location: Athabasca Road, AB-93A, Jasper, AB T0E 1E0, Canada
Contact: +1 780-852-3285
Website: www.alpinevillagejasper.com
Opening Hours: 24 hours, Check-in: 4 PM, Check-out: 11 AM
Description: Alpine Village Jasper offers a distinctive accommodation experience with its rustic cabin resort set in a picturesque landscape across from the Athabasca River. This 2-star hotel is just 2 km from downtown Jasper and 19 km from Marmot Basin ski resort, making it an excellent choice for both summer and winter recreational activities. The resort features simple yet elegant pine log cabins that provide a comfortable and serene environment. Each cabin is equipped with

modern amenities such as free Wi-Fi, satellite TV, mini-fridges, microwaves, and coffeemakers. Select cabins also include separate living spaces, full kitchens, stone fireplaces, and decks with barbecues. Guests can enjoy various facilities including a hot tub, a children's playground, and a spacious deck for relaxation. The Alpine Village Jasper is noted for its tranquil setting and its proximity to local attractions, offering both privacy and convenience.
It operates seasonally, with cabins available from May to October. Free parking is provided for all guests.

HI Jasper
Location: 708 Sleepy Hollow Rd, Jasper, AB T0E 1E0, Canada
Contact: +1 587-870-2395
Website: www.hihostels.ca
Check-in Time: 16:00
Check-out Time: 11:00
Description: HI Jasper, nestled on the outskirts of Jasper, Alberta, offers a welcoming retreat for travelers seeking budget-friendly accommodation surrounded by nature. Situated an 11-minute walk from Jasper train station and 8 km from The Jasper Planetarium, this hostel provides convenient access to both transportation and local attractions.
Accommodation options include shared rooms, ideal for solo travelers or groups, equipped with comfortable beds and shared bathroom facilities. The hostel also features a shared kitchen, allowing guests to prepare their meals, fostering a sense of community among travelers. One of the highlights of HI Jasper is the Sleepy Hollow Café, located on the first floor, offering a cozy ambiance and a selection of refreshments. Guests can enjoy complimentary breakfast and delicious snacks throughout the day. Additionally, the café hosts themed events, such as Dungeons and Dragons night every Thursday at 6 PM, providing entertainment for adventurers and enthusiasts alike.
Free Wi-Fi is available throughout the property, ensuring guests stay connected during their stay. Free parking is also provided for added convenience.

The Crimson Hotel

Located at 200 Connaught Drive in Jasper, Alberta, this conveniently located hotel is a brief stroll from the town's dining establishments. It's also just a short drive from popular attractions like the Jasper Skytram and Marmot Basin ski resort.

The hotel boasts comfortable rooms equipped with complimentary Wi-Fi, flat-screen TVs, minifridges, microwaves, and Keurig coffeemakers for your convenience. Choose an upgraded room for a kitchenette or a suite for a full kitchen and dining area, with select suites offering fireplaces and balconies with mountain views.

Guests can enjoy a range of amenities, including a modern restaurant, an inviting indoor pool, a relaxing hot tub, and a well-equipped fitness center. Additional conveniences such as a guest computer and meeting facilities are also available. For inquiries or bookings, please contact +1 888-414-3559 or visit crimsonjasper.com.

Tekarra Lodge Guide

Location: Highway 93A South, Jasper, Alberta T0E 1E0, Canada
Contact Information: +1 780-852-3058
Website: tekarralodge.com
Opening Hours: Open Daily for check-in from 4:00 PM and check-out by 11:00 AM
Description: Tekarra Lodge, nestled among the evergreen trees of Jasper National Park, offers a unique cabin experience just a short distance from downtown Jasper. The rustic cabins are equipped with kitchenettes or kitchens, pull-out sofas, and wood-burning fireplaces, providing a cozy and comfortable stay. Some cabins even feature separate living and dining areas. The lodge is conveniently located near the Jasper Park Lodge Golf Course.

On-site amenities include a restaurant serving upscale modern dishes prepared with locally sourced ingredients, bike rentals, BBQ facilities, a laundry room, a gift shop, and a children's play area. Please note that the cabins do not have TVs or telephones, allowing guests to fully disconnect and enjoy the tranquility of the natural surroundings.

Bear Hill Lodge Guide
Location: 100 Bonhomme Street, Jasper, Alberta T0E 1E0, Canada
Contact Information: +1 780-852-3209
Website: bearhilllodge.com
Opening Hours: Check-in from 4:00 PM, Check-out by 11:00 AM
Description: Bear Hill Lodge, conveniently situated an 8-minute walk from the Jasper Yellowhead Museum & Archives and 1.1 km from the train station, offers a straightforward yet comfortable stay. The hotel consists of rooms in the main lodge and adjacent cabins, all equipped with TVs and coffeemakers. Some rooms even provide fireplaces and kitchenettes for added convenience. Guests can also opt for suites or 2-bedroom cottages featuring sitting areas and full kitchens.

A continental breakfast buffet is served daily in the main lodge, where guests can also access the Internet, enjoy a sauna or whirlpool, and utilize the laundry facilities. A picnic area is also available on-site for those who prefer to dine outdoors. The hotel offers free parking for guests' convenience.

CANMORE

Canmore, locatled in the heart of the Canadian Rockies just outside Banff National Park, is a vibrant town known for its stunning landscapes and outdoor recreational opportunities. The area around Canmore has a rich history, originally inhabited by the Indigenous peoples of the Stoney Nakoda Nation. The town's development began in the late 19th century with the establishment of coal mines, and it later transitioned to a tourism-based economy after the mines closed in the 1970s. Today, Canmore is a gateway to endless outdoor adventures including hiking, climbing, skiing, and mountain biking. Its proximity to Banff National Park also makes it an ideal base for exploring the broader Rockies region. The town itself offers a charming blend of rustic mountain culture and upscale amenities, with a variety of shops, restaurants, and art galleries that showcase local artistry and craftsmanship.

ATTRACTIONS WITHIN THE TOWN OF CANMORE

Canmore Museum
Location: 902B 7 Ave, Canmore, AB T1W 2B6, Canada
Contact: +1 403-678-2462
Website: www.canmoremuseum.com
Hours: Monday, Thursday to Sunday: 10 AM – 4 PM
- Closed Tuesday and Wednesday

Description: The Canmore Museum, situated in the heart of Canmore, Alberta, offers a detailed exploration of the town's mining history. It showcases a rich collection of photographs, artifacts, and geological specimens that narrate the area's development from a mining community to a vibrant tourist destination. The museum provides an educational experience, highlighting how the 1988 Winter Olympics in Calgary impacted Canmore's growth and popularity.

The museum also features exhibitions on the broader history of the Canadian Rockies, contributing to a deeper understanding of the region's cultural and natural heritage. It is housed in a facility that supports visitor engagement with interactive displays and informative presentations, making it suitable for all ages.

Please note that the Canmore Museum was recently closed from May 21 to June 6, 2024 as a result of an exhibit changeover. Visitors are encouraged to check the website for updates on new exhibitions and any changes in opening hours. Admission fees are kept affordable to ensure accessibility for all visitors, and there is convenient parking nearby.

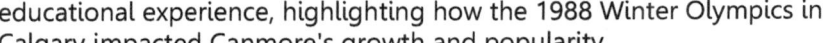

The Caen More ("Big Head" Sculpture)
Location: Canmore, AB T1W 1P3, Canada
Description: The Caen More, also known as the "Big Head" Sculpture, is a distinctive landmark located in Canmore, Alberta. This intriguing artwork, crafted by an Alberta artist and installed in 2008, represents the Scottish Gaelic meaning of Canmore, translating to 'Big Head'. Weighing nine tons, this sculpture is positioned near Policeman's Park and surrounded by a variety of dining options, enhancing its appeal as a cultural and

social focal point in the town. The sculpture occasionally gets adorned with whimsical decorations like knit caps in winter or pirate patches in summer, reflecting the community's playful engagement with the artwork. Visitors to Canmore can enjoy this free attraction at any time, with nearby free parking available approximately 150 meters from the site, making it a convenient and interesting stop during a stroll through the town. Nearby attractions include Canmore Museum and Canmore Engine Bridge, adding to the rich experience of the area.

Canmore Engine Bridge

Location: Spur Line Trail, Canmore, AB T1W 1V9, Canada
Website: www.explorecanmore.ca
Description: The Canmore Engine Bridge, an historical structure built in 1891 by the Canadian Pacific Railway, stands as a prominent landmark in Canmore, Alberta. Originally constructed to support a coal mine rail spur, this bridge is now part of the scenic Bow River loop, offering panoramic views and a peaceful setting ideal for walking, cycling, and photography. Its picturesque surroundings make it a popular spot for both locals and visitors, often serving as the backdrop for family photos and quiet evening walks. The bridge's recent feature in the TV show 'The Last of Us' has further elevated its iconic status. Nearby, visitors can explore additional attractions such as the Riverside Trail, enhancing their experience in the stunning natural landscape of Canmore.

Canmore Nordic Centre

Location: 1988 Olympic Way, Canmore, AB
Contact: +1 403-678-2400
Website: www.albertaparks.ca
Hours: Monday to Sunday: 9 AM – 5:30 PM
Description: Nestled in the picturesque foothills, the Canmore Nordic Centre is renowned for its extensive network of trails suitable for cross-country skiing, mountain biking, and hiking. Established for the 1988 Winter Olympics, this facility continues to offer top-notch recreational opportunities. The centre is dog-friendly, allowing visitors to enjoy the great outdoors with their furry companions. Admission is approximately $9.30 USD, providing access to well-maintained trails that cater to various skill levels, from beginners to advanced enthusiasts. The centre is equipped with rental services for those needing equipment, ensuring a convenient and enjoyable experience. Additional on-site amenities include the Canmore Nordic Centre Provincial Park - Disc Golf Course, Trail Sports sporting goods shop, and Life Works Personal Training. For refreshments, the Cornerstone Catering and Café is available, though some visitors suggest bringing your own lunch for a better dining experience. The facility is ideal for those seeking a day filled with outdoor activities in a scenic setting.

Elevation Place

Location: 700 Railway Ave #100, Canmore, AB T1W 1P4, Canada
Contact: +1 403-678-8920
Website: www.canmore.ca
Opening Hours:
- Monday to Friday: 6 AM – 10 PM
- Saturday to Sunday: 8 AM – 9 PM

Description: Elevation Place is a comprehensive recreation center located in Canmore, Alberta, offering a variety of facilities to cater to fitness and leisure needs. The center includes fitness and cardio rooms, a swimming pool with a kids' area, lazy river, and hot tub, and a significant climbing area. The facility is also home to the Canmore Public Library and Eclipse Coffee Roasters, providing a holistic environment for both physical and mental engagement. Noteworthy features include a waterslide (currently closed) and a climbing wall that attracts both beginners and avid climbers. Elevation Place is celebrated for its well-maintained amenities and the quality of its guest services. The admission fee for adult drop-ins is around $20 USD. The center's versatile offerings make it a popular destination for locals and tourists alike, looking to enjoy a day filled with various activities in a central location. Additional services like the Canmore Mountain Market and Two Brothers Taxi are available on-site, enhancing the convenience for visitors.

Canmore Golf & Curling Club

Location: Pro Shop, 2000 8 Ave, Canmore, AB T1W 1Y2, Canada
Contact: +1 403-678-5959
Website: www.canmoregolf.net
Opening Hours: Monday to Sunday: 7 AM – 9 PM
Description: The Canmore Golf & Curling Club is a premier sports facility in Canmore, Alberta, offering both golf and curling experiences. With a stunning backdrop of the Canadian Rockies, the club provides a picturesque setting that enhances the appeal of playing here. The golf course features lush fairways, quick greens, and a variety of challenges across its holes, making it a favored destination for both casual and serious golfers. For those interested in curling, the club offers facilities and instruction, ideal for beginners or those looking to hone their skills while on vacation. The on-site restaurant, Sandtraps @ The Canmore Golf & Curling Club, serves great food in a beautiful setting, adding to the overall experience. This club is known for its friendly staff and excellent amenities, making it a popular venue for both local and visiting patrons. Non-members can book tee times three days in advance, ensuring accessibility for all visitors.

Quarry Lake Park

Location: Spray Lakes Rd, Canmore, AB T1W 3C2, Canada
Contact: +1 403-678-1500
Website: www.quarrylakecanmore.ca
Opening Hours: Monday to Sunday: 7:30 AM – 6 PM

Description: Quarry Lake Park is a serene recreational area located just outside of Canmore, Alberta, renowned for its picturesque mountain backdrop and a relaxed lake setting. This park is a popular destination for both locals and visitors, offering a range of activities including swimming, picnicking, and walking through its expansive grassy and beach areas. The park is also dog-friendly, featuring a dedicated dog park where pets can roam freely. Additional amenities include public washrooms and picnic tables, enhancing the comfort and convenience for all park-goers. Quarry Lake provides a stunning venue for family outings and social gatherings, with its breathtaking views of the Kananaskis Country mountain range. The park charges for parking, which has been noted by visitors, but the scenic beauty and tranquil atmosphere make it a worthwhile visit.

Avens Gallery

Location: 101-710 8 St, Canmore, AB T1W 2B6, Canada
Contact: +1 403-678-4471
Website: www.theavensgallery.com
Opening Hours:
- Monday to Saturday: 9:30 am – 5:30 pm
- Sunday: 10:00 am – 5:00 pm

Description: Discover a world of artistic wonder at Avens Gallery, located in the heart of Canmore, Alberta, Canada. This captivating art gallery showcases a diverse collection of stunning artwork, providing visitors with an immersive experience into the realm of creativity and expression.

Step into Avens Gallery and be greeted by an array of amazing art pieces adorning the space, each one carefully curated to delight and inspire. From paintings to sculptures, Avens offers a breathtaking selection of artwork that captivates the senses and sparks the imagination.

The gallery's atmosphere is inviting and welcoming, with friendly and knowledgeable staff on hand to assist and guide visitors through their artistic journey. Whether you're a seasoned art enthusiast or a novice admirer, Avens Gallery offers something for everyone, catering to diverse tastes and preferences.

One of the highlights of Avens Gallery is its dedication to showcasing the work of talented artists, providing a platform for both established and emerging creatives to share their vision with the world.

Carter-Ryan Gallery

Location: 705 8 St, Canmore, AB T1W 2B2, Canada
Contact Information: +1 403-621-1000
Website: www.carter-ryan.com
Opening Hours:

- Mon: 10 AM – 5 PM, Saturday: 10 AM – 5 PM, Sun: 10 AM – 3 PM,
- Closed on Tuesday, Wednesday, Thursday, and Friday

Description: The Carter-Ryan Gallery in Canmore, Alberta, is a contemporary art space featuring a vibrant collection of paintings and wood carvings by Canadian artist Jason Carter. The gallery offers a visually stimulating experience with its modern and sleek design that showcases colorful and dynamic artworks. Each piece reflects the cultural and natural heritage of the region, making it a significant cultural spot in Canmore.

The gallery is open to the public with no admission fee required, allowing free access to all visitors. It operates with specific open days, focusing on weekend visitors, which makes it a perfect cultural stop for both local and touring art enthusiasts. The gallery also serves as a theatrical venue, occasionally hosting live productions which add a dynamic layer to its cultural offerings.

The Ken Hoehn Gallery
Location: 729 8 St #104, Canmore, AB T1W 2B2, Canada
Contact: +1 403-675-6677
Website: www.kenhoehn.ca
Opening Hours:
- Monday to Thursday: 10:00 am – 6:00 pm
- Friday & Saturday: 10:00 am – 8:00 pm
- Sunday: 9:00 am – 5:00 pm

Description: The Ken Hoehn Gallery, nestled in the heart of Canmore, Alberta, offers a captivating collection of nature-inspired photographs that celebrate the beauty of Canada's wilderness. Founded by acclaimed photographer Ken Hoehn, this gallery is a testament to his passion for capturing the essence of the natural world. Step inside and immerse yourself in a world of stunning imagery, where each photograph tells a unique story of the Canadian landscape. From majestic mountains to tranquil forests, Ken's artwork captures the awe-inspiring beauty of nature in all its forms. Whether you're an avid art collector or simply appreciate the wonders of the great outdoors, the gallery's diverse collection is sure to captivate your imagination.
Beyond its impressive artwork, The Ken Hoehn Gallery offers visitors a personalized experience, with Ken himself often on hand to share the stories behind his photographs. His deep connection to the natural world shines through in every piece, offering viewers a deeper appreciation for the landscapes that surround us.
Whether you're seeking to add a touch of natural beauty to your home or simply wish to immerse yourself in the splendor of Canada's wilderness, a visit to The Ken Hoehn Gallery is sure to inspire and delight.

Canadian Rockies Earth Science Resource Centre

Location: 829 10 St #111, Canmore, AB T1W 0C3, Canada
Contact: +1 403-678-5822 | **Website:** www.canrock.ca
Opening Hours: Saturday: 10:00 am – 5:00 pm
Description: The Canadian Rockies Earth Science Resource Centre offers an immersive journey into the geological wonders of the region. Located in Canmore, Alberta, this museum showcases captivating exhibits on various aspects of geoscience, from the formation of the Rockies to the exploration of mineral resources. Visitors can explore informative displays that delve into topics such as geology, oil and gas exploration, and the Canadian Geological Survey's contributions to understanding the region's geological history. The center provides a unique learning experience suitable for all ages, with knowledgeable staff on hand to offer engaging tours and insights. Admission fees are affordable, making it an excellent value for families and individuals interested in the Earth sciences. With its passionate dedication to education and exploration, the Canadian Rockies Earth Science Resource Centre is a must-visit destination for anyone fascinated by the natural world.

Grassi Lakes
Location: Bow Valley Wildland Provincial Park, Canmore, Alberta, Canada
Description: Grassi Lakes Trail, situated in the picturesque Bow Valley Wildland Provincial Park near Canmore, Alberta, is a 1.1-kilometer out-and-back trail that ascends 106 meters through moderate terrain. This trail is perfect for hikers of all abilities and is celebrated for its breathtaking forest views, serene lakes, and diverse wildlife. As a year-round accessible route, the trail is most enjoyable from May to October. The trail winds through a designated Wildlife Corridor, enhancing both the protection of local fauna and the safety of hikers. It's important for visitors to stick to marked paths and to carry bear spray due to frequent bear sightings. Additionally, while the area is popular among climbers who frequent the cliffs around the lakes, hikers are advised to keep a safe distance unless properly equipped for climbing.
Construction Advisory: From May 21 to July 31, 2024, Grassi Lakes trails will undergo drainage improvements to address erosion issues. During this period, there may be temporary, intermittent closures. Visitors should consult the Alberta Parks website or contact the

Kananaskis Information Line at (403) 678-0760 for the latest updates. Despite construction, access to the lakes via alternative trails might still be possible.

Trail Options:
- **Easy Route:** Suitable for families, this gentle incline leads to the stunning turquoise waters of Grassi Lakes.
- **More Challenging Route:** Offers a steeper trek through wooded areas, past a waterfall, and features striking views of Canmore and the Bow Valley.

Hiking Time: Approximately 1 to 2 hours for the complete 4 km (2.5 mi) hike.

Transportation: Roam Transit's new Route 12 service offers connectivity from downtown Canmore to the Grassi Lakes trailhead, including stops at Quarry Lake and the Canmore Nordic Centre. This service is available on Fridays, Saturdays, Sundays, and Statutory holiday Mondays from May through September. Impressively, all local Canmore routes are free of charge.

For additional details on the Roam Transit services, visit roamtransit.com.

Ha Ling Peak Trail

Location: Bow Valley Wildland Provincial Park, Canmore, Alberta, Canada

Description: The Ha Ling Peak Trail offers a challenging yet rewarding outdoor experience for hikers in the stunning Bow Valley Wildland Provincial Park. Spanning 7.4 kilometers as an out-and-back route, this trail boasts an elevation gain of 755 meters, making it suitable for experienced hikers seeking an exhilarating adventure. Renowned for its breathtaking views and diverse terrain, the trail attracts outdoor enthusiasts year-round for activities such as hiking, rock climbing, and snowshoeing. The trail begins at a designated parking lot and winds through the picturesque Canadian Rocky Mountain forest before ascending onto open rock faces and fewer  trees. During the summer months, the trail is typically clear, but hikers are advised to carry proper climbing equipment, especially for the higher sections. As the trail ascends, hikers are treated to panoramic views of the surrounding landscape, with opportunities to marvel at the town of Canmore from the ridge.

The trail features challenging sections, including steep climbs and rocky scrambles, which require caution and endurance. Hikers are encouraged to take breaks along the way to appreciate the stunning vistas and recharge. The trail is busiest on warm weekend days during the summer, so early arrival is recommended to avoid crowds. During winter, access to the trailhead may be affected by road closures, adding distance to the route.

Descending the trail can also pose challenges, particularly against traffic moving uphill. In winter conditions, the trail presents a difficult mountaineering endeavor and should only be attempted by experienced hikers. Additionally, there is an avalanche hazard in the area during winter months. It is very windy and cold at the

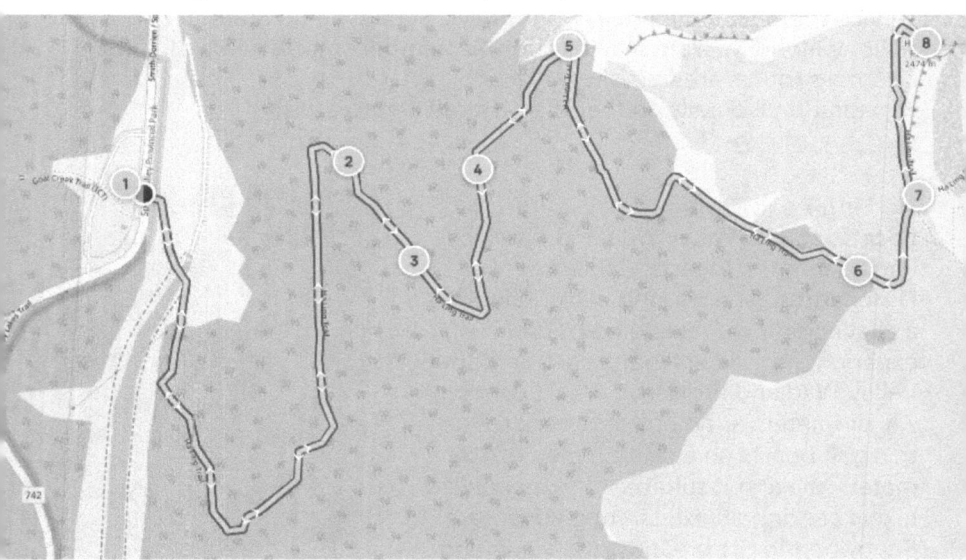

NEARBY CANMORE ATTRACTION

BOW VALLEY PROVINCIAL PARK - KANANASKIS COUNTRY

Location: 800 Railway Ave #201, Canmore, AB T1W 1P1, Canada
Contact Information: +1 403-678-0760
Website: https://www.albertaparks.ca/parks/kananaskis/
Opening Hours: Sunday to Monday: 8 AM – 11 PM
Description: Bow Valley Provincial Park, nestled in the scenic Kananaskis Country near Canmore, Alberta, offers a tranquil escape into nature with fewer tourists compared to more frequented sites like Banff and Lake Louise. This park provides a plethora of activities including mountain hiking, paddle boating, and wildlife viewing, with possible sightings of mountain goats and bears.

Visitors can explore a variety of trails ranging from easy strolls to challenging hikes, leading through diverse landscapes of mountains, waterfalls, lakes, and valleys. The park is known for its accessible yet rugged terrain, with some areas under road construction, suggesting a readiness for more rugged travel conditions.

Significant nearby attractions include Grassi Lake, known for its serene beauty and less-trodden paths. Bow Valley Provincial Park's vast area and rich natural offerings make it an ideal location for outdoor enthusiasts looking to immerse themselves in Alberta's wilderness without the heavy crowds found at more commercialized national parks.

Kananaskis Country Conservation Pass
Website: https://conservationpass.alberta.ca/kcp
Location: Available online and at various visitor information centres within Kananaskis Country and Bow Valley, including Barrier, Elbow, Peter Lougheed, and William Watson Lodge, as well as the Canmore Nordic Centre Day Lodge.

Visitors planning to park at provincial park and public land sites within Kananaskis Country and the Bow Valley require a Conservation Pass. This pass is crucial for maintaining and enhancing the park facilities and conservation efforts in these areas.

Purchase Options and Costs:
Personal Vehicles:
- **Day Pass:** $15 USD (covers one vehicle)
- **Annual Pass:** $90 USD (registers up to 3 vehicles)

Commercial Vehicles (15 people or less):
- **Day Pass:** $22.50 USD
- **Annual Pass:** $135 USD
- *Applicable to shuttles, taxis, and small group transport.*

Commercial Vehicles (more than 15 people):
- **Day Pass:** $30 USD
- **Annual Pass:** $180 USD
- *Applicable to large group transport and coach buses.*

Additional Information: Passes can be purchased online, where you can also register your vehicle's license plate. Alternatively, passes are available for purchase in-person or via Wi-Fi at designated visitor information centres throughout the region. Each pass covers all passengers within the vehicle and any trailers attached. Passes are vehicle-specific and cannot be transferred to another vehicle.

Kananaskis Country Summer Events
Location: Bow Valley Amphitheatre - Bow Valley Provincial Park
Description: This summer, Bow Valley Provincial Park's Amphitheatre hosts a series of musical theatre performances designed to educate and entertain about the wildlife in Kananaskis Country. These family-friendly events merge captivating storytelling with music, enhancing your understanding of local ecosystems.

General Information:
Dates: June 14 - September 2, 2024
Time: 7:30 PM (specific times for each event may vary, check local listings)
Duration: 50 minutes for each performance

Admission: Free (a Kananaskis Conservation Pass is required for vehicle parking)
Event Details:
1. **Dungeons & Dragonflies**: Learn about aquatic insects through this engaging performance. Suitable for all ages, though children under 12 must be accompanied by an adult. No pets allowed in the amphitheater.
2. **Nasty Business**: Explore the less-loved 'nasty' creatures of Kananaskis with an entertaining mix of music and facts.
3. **Finding Fawn**: Discover the life and challenges of deer in Kananaskis through this informative musical performance.
4. **Star Bears:** Dive into the world of bears and the importance of their conservation.

Kananaskis Country Trails

Kananaskis Country offers a variety of trails suitable for various activities year-round, allowing visitors to explore the natural beauty of the area through hiking, biking, e-biking, fat biking, and horseback riding. The trails cater to all levels of outdoor enthusiasts, from casual hikers to adventurous bikers, providing a diverse range of experiences in the scenic landscapes of the Canadian Rockies.

Bow River Interpretive
Location: Between Whitefish Day Use Area and Bow Valley Campground, Kananaskis Country, Alberta, Canada
Description: The Bow River Interpretive Trail is a scenic pathway that runs alongside the Bow River, connecting the Whitefish Day Use Area to the Bow Valley Campground. This trail offers a tranquil hiking experience with picturesque views of the river and surrounding forested areas.
Trail Details:
Group Size Limit: Up to 35 people
Length: 2.1 km one-way
Activities: Hiking
Status: Open

Bow Valley Paved
Length: 4.2 km one-way
Activities: Hiking, E-bikes, Fat Biking, Biking
Status: Open

Description: Navigate a paved pathway that winds through undulating landscapes, providing lovely vistas of both meadows and woodlands.

Elk Flats
Length: 1.9 km one-way
Activities: Hiking
Status: Open
Description: Traverse through a blend of forested areas and open meadows, enjoying the natural scenery along the way.

Flowing Water Interpretive
Length: 2.0 km return
Activities: Hiking
Status: Open
Description: This route offers impressive views of the mountains and the Kananaskis River. Features include a lookout point over a beaver pond and educational signs about the hydrological cycle.

Heart Creek Interpretive
Length: 1.3 km one-way
Activities: Hiking
Status: Open
Description: Follow a narrow canyon creek across seven bridges, leading to a secluded waterfall.

Jewell Pass
Length: 2.9 km one-way
Activities: Hiking, Biking
Status: Open
Description: Starting from Barrier Dam, this 2.9 km trail winds past the serene Jewell Falls and offers stunning views of Barrier Lake. The trail can be accessed by crossing Barrier Dam and taking the Stoney Trail south to the turnoff. It is commonly paired with the Prairie View Trail for a full loop experience.

Many Springs Interpretive
Length: 1.3 km
Activities: Hiking
Status: Open

Description: Circle a unique wetland basin, rich with rare plant species. An observation deck allows for viewing of the springs, with interpretative signage explaining the local ecosystem.

Middle Lake Interpretive
Length: 2.0 km | **Activities:** Hiking | **Status:** Open
Description: This trail gently winds through forests and meadows, skirting the edges of Middle Lake.

Montane Interpretive
Length: 1.5 km
Activities: Hiking
Status: Open
Description: Experience a tranquil walk through forests and meadows, with educational signs that provide insights into the montane forest ecosystem.

Moraine Interpretive
Length: 1.1 km one-way
Activities: Hiking
Status: Open
Description: This scenic trail runs along the top of a glacial ridge, offering expansive mountain views, complemented by signs that explain the glacial features of the area.

Prairie View
Length: 6.6 km one-way to viewpoint
Activities: Hiking, Fat Biking, Biking
Notes: Clear front side, snowy and icy sections on the backside as of May 30th
Status: Open
Description: Known as the Barrier Fire Lookout trail, this path switchbacks up an old forestry road to a dramatic southern viewpoint over Barrier Lake. From there, hikers can either head to the Barrier Fire Lookout for views over the Bow Valley or descend towards Jewell Pass along a less distinct path that clarifies as it enters the forest.

Quaite Creek
Length: 5.7 km one-way to Jewell Pass
Activities: Hiking, Fat Biking, Horseback Riding, Biking
Notes: Snow at higher elevations as of May 30th

Status: Open
Description: This enjoyable route provides access to the Heart Creek Interpretive Trail just 0.8 km from the starting point. The Quaite Valley Backcountry Campground lies 5.7 km in, with the path continuing to Jewell Pass and connecting with the Jewell Pass Trail and Prairie View Trail.

Stoney
Length: 22.5 km one-way
Activities: Hiking, E-bikes, Fat Biking, Horseback Riding, Biking, Snowshoeing
Status: Closed as of June, 2024
This is a long, open trail following the power line. Equestrian camping is available at Jewell Bay Backcountry Campground.
Stoney Trail is closed annually from April 15-June 15, from (and including) Jewel Bay Campground south to Lorette Creek.

Trail Conditions (as of May 30): Trails are generally dry, with lingering snow at higher elevations and shaded areas. Visitors should be prepared for rapid changes in weather, especially rain at lower elevations that may turn into snow at higher altitudes.
Key Advisories:
Closures:
- **Lady Macdonald and Cougar Creek Canyon:** Closed due to construction.
- **Pigeon Mountain & West Wind Valley:** Closed Dec 1 - Jun 15 for elk and bighorn sheep winter protection.
- **Mt. Allan / Centennial Ridge Trail:** Closed Apr 1 - Jun 21 for bighorn sheep birthing.
- **Stoney Trail:** Closed Apr 15 - Jun 15 from Jewell Bay Backcountry Campground to Evan-Thomas Provincial Recreation Area boundary.

Bear Activity: Notable at YMCA Camp Chief Hector.
Construction: Noted at Quaite Valley Backcountry Campground.

Adventure and Tours in Canmore

Snowy Owl Sled Dog Tours Inc
Location: 829 10 St, Canmore, AB T1W 0C3, Canada
Contact: +1 403-678-4369
Website: www.snowyowltours.com
Hours: Monday to Thursday: 10 AM – 4 PM, Friday to Sunday: Closed
Description: Snowy Owl Sled Dog Tours Inc offers an unforgettable adventure amidst the breathtaking Canadian Rockies. As a premier dogsled ride service, visitors are treated to a thrilling journey led by expert guides and a team of energetic sled dogs. The experience is suitable for all ages, with options for both instructor-driven and self-driven sleds. The tour takes guests through picturesque trails, providing opportunities to interact with the friendly and well-cared-for sled dogs.

Alpine Helicopters Inc.
Location: 91 Bow Valley Trail, Canmore, AB T1W 1N8, Canada
Contact: +1 403-678-4802
Website: www.alpinehelicopter.com
Opening Hours: Monday to Sunday: 8 AM – 4 PM
Description: Alpine Helicopters Inc. offers breathtaking sightseeing tours over the stunning landscapes of the Canadian Rockies. As a leading sightseeing tour agency, Alpine Helicopters provides unforgettable aerial experiences, allowing visitors to marvel at majestic mountains, glaciers, lakes, and other notable landmarks. Their fleet of modern helicopters ensures both safety and comfort, with knowledgeable pilots providing informative commentary throughout the tour.

Canmore Cave Tours
Location: 129 Bow Meadows Crescent #101, Canmore, AB T1W 2W8
Contact: +1 403-678-8819
Website: www.canmorecavetours.com
Opening Hours: Monday to Sunday: 9 AM – 5 PM
Description: Canmore Cave Tours offers thrilling underground adventures in the Rat's Nest Cave, a protected site located on private land. Access to the cave is restricted to guided tours led by knowledgeable and friendly staff. The tours provide participants with a unique opportunity to explore the cave's fascinating geological formations, learn about its history, and experience the excitement of caving.

YOHO NATIONAL PARK

Location: Improvement District No. 9, AB, Canada
Phone number: 250-343-6783
Email address: yoho.info@pc.gc.ca
Website: https://parks.canada.ca/pn-np/bc/yoho

Yoho National Park, established in 1886, is renowned for its complex geology and fossil sites, notably the Burgess Shale, which contains some of the best-preserved fossils of Cambrian marine life. The park's name, Yoho, comes from a Cree word expressing awe, which reflects the stunning natural beauty of the area. Though smaller and less developed than its neighboring parks, Yoho offers a quiet retreat into nature. Key attractions include the Takakkaw Falls, one of Canada's tallest waterfalls, and Emerald Lake. The park's rugged terrain and extensive trail network attract hikers and climbers from around the world.

Yoho National Park, a bastion of natural wonders, is renowned for its majestic peaks, historic waterways, and vibrant community. The park features 28 peaks over 3,000 meters, creating a dramatic landscape of rock walls and waterfalls. The park is located within the Rocky Mountains on the western slope of the Continental Divide in southeastern British Columbia, shares borders with Kootenay National Park to the south and Banff National Park to the east in Alberta, forming a vast wilderness area that is a haven for outdoor enthusiasts. Here's a guide to the park's notable points of interest:

Village of Field
Description: Nestled in the 1880s as a Canadian Pacific Railway siding, Field is now the heart of Yoho, offering mountain hospitality, unique guesthouses, shops, and dining. The Yoho Visitor Centre here provides insights and guidance for exploring the park.

Emerald Lake
Description: Known for its stunning mountain and wildflower views, Emerald Lake allows for leisure activities like picnicking and canoeing around its vibrant waters.
Facilities and Activities: Accessible paths, washrooms, picnic areas, viewpoints, canoeing, and dining.
Trail: Lakeshore Trail - 5.2 km, minimal elevation, offering a gentle, scenic walk.

Natural Bridge
Description: The Natural Bridge is a striking geological formation located within Yoho National Park. This natural rock bridge spans the powerful flow of the Kicking Horse River, showcasing the dynamic forces of water erosion and natural architecture. It is easily accessible from the Trans-Canada Highway and offers a picturesque stop on the journey between Golden and Banff.
Visitors can enjoy the view from several vantage points around the bridge, making it a perfect spot for photography and nature observation. The area around Natural Bridge is also equipped with basic amenities like restrooms, although visitors should bring their own hand sanitizers as there is no running water available for handwashing.

Kicking Horse River
Description: Trace the path of this Canadian Heritage River, known for its expansive, braided gravel flats and dramatic history.
Points of Interest: Follow the river to Natural Bridge and Wapta Falls, experiencing the park's rugged terrain.

Takakkaw Falls
Location: Columbia-Shuswap, BC V0A 1G0, Canada
Description: Takakkaw Falls, located in Yoho National Park, is an iconic waterfall renowned for its impressive height and stunning natural surroundings. Towering majestically, the falls offer visitors a breathtaking sight amidst a sprawling park landscape. Low-key hiking trails provide close views of the cascading waters, making it a popular destination for nature enthusiasts and photographers alike.

Situated within the park, Takakkaw Falls is surrounded by picturesque scenery, creating a serene atmosphere for visitors to immerse themselves in the beauty of nature. The falls can be accessed easily, allowing visitors to experience its grandeur firsthand. During warmer days, the spray from the falls can be felt from a distance, adding to the immersive experience.

Adjacent to Takakkaw Falls is a walk-in campground and the HI-Whiskey Jack Hostel, providing convenient accommodation options for those wishing to stay close to this natural wonder. The campground offers well-maintained facilities, ensuring a comfortable and enjoyable stay for visitors. Additionally, carts are available to transport belongings from the parking lot to the campground, enhancing the convenience for campers.

Takakkaw Falls is a must-see attraction for anyone exploring the Rockies, offering a memorable experience that showcases the beauty of Canada's natural landscapes. It is accessible via Yoho Valley Road with restrictions for larger vehicles.

Yoho Valley
Description: The valley extends from Takakkaw Falls through various landscapes, leading to Laughing Falls, Twin Falls, and beyond.
Activities: Back-country camping, hiking, and stays at Stanley Mitchell Hut.

Spiral Tunnels viewpoint
Description: Observe trains navigating the engineering marvel of the Spiral Tunnels, and learn about the historic Kicking Horse Pass.
Facilities: Viewpoints and exhibits detailing the construction and history.

Kicking Horse Pass National Historic Site
Description: This crucial pass plays a historic role in connecting the Trans-Canada Highway and Canadian Pacific Railway across the Continental Divide.

Wapta Falls
Description: Experience the largest waterfall on the Kicking Horse River through a scenic forest hike.
Trail: Wapta Falls Trail - 4.6 km, 30 m elevation gain.
Description: The trailhead is conveniently located at Wapta Falls Trail Head Pk,

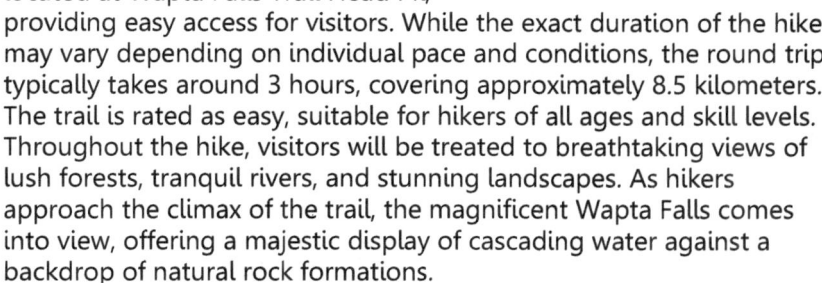

providing easy access for visitors. While the exact duration of the hike may vary depending on individual pace and conditions, the round trip typically takes around 3 hours, covering approximately 8.5 kilometers. The trail is rated as easy, suitable for hikers of all ages and skill levels. Throughout the hike, visitors will be treated to breathtaking views of lush forests, tranquil rivers, and stunning landscapes. As hikers approach the climax of the trail, the magnificent Wapta Falls comes into view, offering a majestic display of cascading water against a backdrop of natural rock formations.
During the winter months, exploring Wapta Falls presents a unique opportunity to witness the beauty of the frozen landscape. Hikers are advised to come prepared with appropriate gear, including spikes for traction on icy trails.

Burgess Shale fossil guided hikes
Description: Engage with Earth's distant past on guided hikes to significant fossil sites, offering a hands-on experience with prehistoric life.
Booking Information: Advanced booking required for these educational tours.

Sherbrooke Lake Trail

Description: Sherbrooke Lake Trail, nestled in the scenic Yoho National Park, offers a 9.3-kilometer out-and-back journey that is considered moderately challenging. With an elevation gain of 319 meters, it typically takes about 2 hours and 45 minutes to complete. This trail is highly popular for bird watching, cross-country skiing, hiking, and snowshoeing, attracting a variety of outdoor enthusiasts. The trail is accessible from May through October, providing a rich, natural escape for visitors. In winter, the trail may be covered in deep snow and blizzard conditions, making navigation challenging without proper equipment.

Meeting of the waters confluent

Location: Yoho Valley Rd, Field, BC V0A 1G0, Canada

Description: The Meeting of the Waters Confluent offers a unique natural spectacle where two different colors of water merge into one, creating a mesmerizing sight that captivates visitors. Located along Yoho Valley Road in Field, British Columbia, this scenic spot provides a serene and relaxing experience for nature lovers. Accessed easily from the road, the viewpoint allows visitors to witness the convergence of two rivers, each displaying distinct colors as they join together. The small parking area provides convenience for visitors, and from there, a short but somewhat steep and gravelly path leads down to the confluence.

While the view may vary depending on the time of day and lighting conditions, the Meeting of the Waters remains a must-stop destination for travelers exploring the Yoho National Park area. Picnic tables near the parking area offer a place to relax and enjoy the surroundings, making it an ideal spot for a brief stopover on the way to other attractions like Takakkaw Falls.

Laughing falls

Location: Columbia-Shuswap A, BC, Canada
Description: Laughing Falls, nestled in the breathtaking landscape of Columbia-Shuswap, is a captivating tourist attraction renowned for its natural beauty and serene ambiance. This picturesque waterfall, surrounded by pristine wilderness, offers visitors an unforgettable experience in the heart of nature.

Accessible via a well-maintained trail, Laughing Falls is an ideal side stop for those already visiting the nearby Takakkaw Falls parking lot and looking to extend their adventure. The hike to Laughing Falls takes approximately an hour one way and is characterized by an easy-to-follow trail, with only one steep section. Along the way, hikers can enjoy the scenic beauty of the surrounding landscape, making stops at points of interest like Point Lace Falls.

While the hike may be moderately long, the reward at the end is truly worth it. Visitors are greeted by the breathtaking sight of Laughing Falls cascading gracefully amidst the tranquil wilderness. The serene atmosphere and the soothing sound of rushing water create a sense of peace and tranquility, making Laughing Falls a perfect spot for relaxation and rejuvenation.

Additional Services and Facilities

Emerald Lake Canoe Rentals & The Boathouse Trading Co.
Location: 1A Emerald Lake Rd, Field, BC V0A 1G0, Canada
Contact: +1 250-343-6000
Website: www.boathousetradingco.com
Description: Emerald Lake Canoe Rentals & The Boathouse Trading Co. offers a delightful experience for outdoor enthusiasts visiting the scenic Emerald Lake in British Columbia's Yoho National Park. While temporarily closed, this establishment typically provides equipment rental services and a charming lakeside atmosphere for visitors to enjoy.

Situated amidst the captivating beauty of Yoho National Park, Emerald Lake is renowned for its crystal-clear waters and stunning mountain scenery. Emerald Lake Canoe Rentals offers visitors the opportunity to explore this natural wonder by renting canoes to paddle across the tranquil waters.

The Boathouse Trading Co., adjacent to the rental facility, provides a welcoming atmosphere where visitors can gather and prepare for their lake adventure. While awaiting the reopening, guests can anticipate a range of amenities and services aimed at enhancing their experience at Emerald Lake.

Visitors can expect friendly and knowledgeable staff who are dedicated to ensuring a memorable experience on the lake.

Kingmik Dog Sled Tours
Location: 16430 Hwy 1A, Lake Louise, AB T0L 1E0, Canada
Contact: +1 855-482-4592
Website: www.kingmikdogsledtours.com
Opening Hours: Monday to Friday: 8 AM – 6 PM, Saturday: 8 AM – 8 PM
Description: Kingmik Dog Sled Tours, situated in the picturesque Lake Louise, Alberta, offers visitors an exhilarating experience amidst the stunning Canadian Rockies. The attraction provides an authentic dog sledding adventure led by experienced mushers and their enthusiastic team of sled dogs.

Upon arrival, guests are warmly greeted at the tour center and introduced to the friendly and well-trained sled dogs. The journey begins with panoramic views of the surrounding mountains and forests as guests glide through pristine snow-covered trails. The sight of the dogs working in harmony adds to the excitement, creating an unforgettable experience.

Throughout the tour, knowledgeable guides share insights into the history of dog sledding and the unique bond between musher and dog. Guests have the opportunity to interact with the dogs, learning about their breeds and personalities.

Kingmik Dog Sled Tours prioritizes eco-friendly practices, providing guests with a sustainable adventure that minimizes environmental impact. Reservations are recommended due to high demand, and visitors are advised to check the website for updates on tour availability.

As part of Lake Louise's attractions, Kingmik Dog Sled Tours offers an opportunity to connect with nature and experience the spirit of the Canadian wilderness in a memorable and immersive way.

Kicking Horse Campground

Location: 29 Yoho Valley Rd, Field, BC V0A 1G0, Canada
Contact: +1 877-737-3783
Website: www.parks.canada.ca
Opening Hours: Check-in Time: 2:00 PM, Check-out Time: 11:00 AM
Description: Kicking Horse Campground, nestled in the serene wilderness of Field, British Columbia, offers a tranquil retreat for nature lovers and outdoor enthusiasts. Located within Yoho National Park, this campground provides an ideal base for exploring the stunning landscapes and outdoor activities the area has to offer.

The campground features well-maintained campsites suitable for tents and RVs, offering a range of amenities to ensure a comfortable stay amidst nature. Each campsite is equipped with picnic tables and fire pits, providing the perfect setting for enjoying meals and gathering around the campfire under the starry night sky.

Guests can enjoy a variety of recreational activities, including hiking, wildlife viewing, and photography, with numerous trails and scenic viewpoints accessible directly from the campground. Nearby attractions such as Emerald Lake, Takakkaw Falls, and the Burgess Shale Fossil Beds offer further opportunities for exploration and discovery.

For those seeking adventure, Kicking Horse Campground serves as a convenient starting point for outdoor pursuits such as rock climbing, mountain biking, and whitewater rafting. Guided tours and interpretive programs are available seasonally, providing educational insights into the park's natural and cultural heritage.

Reservations are recommended, especially during peak seasons, to secure a campsite. Visitors should note that the campground is a popular destination, with limited availability for walk-in campers.

HI Yoho National Park, Whiskey Jack Wilderness Hostel
Location: Yoho National Park of Canada, Yoho Valley Rd, Columbia-Shuswap, BC V0A 1G0, Canada
Contact: +1 778-328-2220
Website: www.hihostels.ca
Opening Hours:
- Check-in Time: 5:00 PM
- Check-out Time: 10:00 AM

Description: Set amidst the secluded forests of Yoho National Park, HI Yoho National Park, Whiskey Jack Wilderness Hostel offers a rustic retreat for travelers seeking solace in nature. Located just a 13-minute walk from the awe-inspiring Takakkaw Falls, this seasonal hostel provides a serene getaway from the hustle and bustle of city life.
The hostel features cozy accommodations in a wilderness setting, providing an authentic back-to-nature experience for guests. With a range of amenities including free Wi-Fi, complimentary breakfast, and ample free parking, visitors can enjoy modern comforts amidst the rugged wilderness.
Surrounded by towering trees and scenic trails, the hostel offers opportunities for hiking, wildlife viewing, and photography right at its doorstep. Guests can explore nearby attractions such as Emerald Lake, Natural Bridge, and the Burgess Shale Fossil Beds, each offering unique insights into the park's natural beauty and geological history.

Emerald Lake Lodge
Location: 1 Emerald Lake Rd, Field, BC V0A 1G0, Canada
Contact: +1 250-343-6321 | **Website:** www.crmr.com
Check-in Time: 16:00, **Check-out Time:** 11:00
Description: Nestled in the picturesque landscape of Yoho National Park, Emerald Lake Lodge offers a tranquil retreat amidst the stunning beauty of British Columbia's wilderness. This 4-star hotel provides guests with a serene getaway, surrounded by pristine nature and breathtaking views.
The lodge features rustic yet cozy accommodations, with options for lakeside rooms providing unparalleled vistas of Emerald Lake. While some guests have noted that the rooms may feel a bit outdated, many appreciate the charm and character of the lodge's architecture. Each

room is equipped with a fireplace, offering a cozy ambiance perfect for relaxation after a day of exploring.
Guests can dine at the Mount Burgess Dining Room, where they can enjoy delicious meals accompanied by panoramic views of the surrounding mountains. The menu offers a variety of options, with highlights including the chicken main dish, praised for its flavor and quality.
While the lodge provides a peaceful escape from the hustle and bustle of city life, guests should note that there is limited cell service and no Wi-Fi in the rooms. However, this only enhances the opportunity to disconnect and immerse oneself in the tranquility of nature.
In addition to its accommodations and dining options, Emerald Lake Lodge offers amenities such as a hot tub, providing guests with the opportunity to unwind and soak in the natural beauty of the area. Shuttle services are available to transport guests from the parking area to the lodge reception, ensuring convenience and ease of access.

Truffle Pigs Bistro & Lodge
Location: 100 Center Street, Field, BC V0A 1G0, Canada
Contact: +1 250-343-6303
Opening Hours: Monday to Sunday: 11:00 AM – 9:00 PM
Description: Truffle Pigs Bistro & Lodge offers a cozy retreat in the heart of Yoho National Park, surrounded by the majestic Rocky Mountains. Located just three miles from the Canadian Rocky Mountain Parks World Heritage Site, this lodge and bistro provide visitors with a comfortable and relaxing atmosphere to unwind after a day of exploration.
The lodge features a rustic yet inviting ambiance, with accommodations designed to provide guests with a comfortable and memorable stay. While some guests have noted that the rooms may feel a bit outdated, many appreciate the charm and warmth of the lodge's interior. Each room is equipped with amenities to ensure a pleasant stay, including free Wi-Fi and complimentary breakfast.
The on-site bistro offers a delightful dining experience, serving up a variety of creative dishes made with locally sourced ingredients. Guests can enjoy a range of options, including vegan and vegetarian choices, in a relaxed and welcoming setting. The restaurant also offers its own chocolate, available for purchase in the souvenir shop.
While staying at Truffle Pigs Bistro & Lodge, guests can take advantage of the lodge's convenient location to explore the natural beauty of Yoho National Park.

Cathedral Mountain Lodge
Location: 1 Yoho Valley Rd, Field, BC V0A 1G0, Canada
Contact: +1 250-343-6442
Website: www.cathedralmountainlodge.com
Opening Hours: Monday to Sunday: Check-in at 16:00, Check-out at 11:00
Description: Cathedral Mountain Lodge offers a serene retreat in the picturesque Yoho Valley of British Columbia, Canada. Situated by the tranquil riverbanks, the lodge provides an idyllic setting for relaxation and exploration. Guests can choose from authentic cabins featuring lovely furnishings and spacious interiors, ensuring a comfortable stay amidst nature's beauty. The lodge's restaurant area provides an excellent dining experience, with options to enjoy meals outdoors amidst breathtaking views. The food is renowned for its excellence, complemented by top-notch service. Guests can savor delicious meals while soaking in the serene ambiance of the surroundings. The lodge's stylish vibe and attentive staff enhance the overall experience, making it a preferred destination for travelers seeking tranquility and natural beauty. Whether relaxing by the riverbanks with a bottle of wine or exploring the nearby Yoho Park and Lake Louise/Moraine Lake areas, Cathedral Mountain Lodge offers a memorable stay in the heart of nature.

Canadian Rockies Inn
Location: 100 Center Street, Field, BC V0A 1G0, Canada
Contact: +1 250-343-6303
Website: www.trufflepigs.com
Opening Hours:
- Monday to Sunday: Check-in at 16:00, Check-out at 11:00

Description: Truffle Pigs Bistro & Lodge, located in the charming town of Field within Yoho National Park, offers a delightful combination of dining and lodging experiences. The bistro boasts a diverse menu featuring creative dishes crafted with locally sourced ingredients, catering to various dietary preferences including vegan and vegetarian options. Guests can savor their meals in a cozy and inviting atmosphere, with both indoor and outdoor seating available. The lodge provides comfortable accommodations, allowing guests to unwind after a day of exploration in the park. The rustic charm of the lodge complements the natural beauty of its surroundings, offering a serene retreat amidst the Canadian Rockies. Additionally, the bistro's souvenir shop offers locally made chocolates, adding a sweet touch to the overall experience. Truffle Pigs Bistro & Lodge is a perfect destination for travelers seeking a memorable culinary and lodging experience in the heart of Yoho National Park.

Cilantro On The Lake
Location: 1 Emerald Lake Rd, Field, BC V0A 1G0, Canada
Contact: +1 250-343-6321 | **Website:** www.cilantroonthelake.com
Opening Hours: Wednesday to Sunday: 2–8 PM, Monday and Tuesday: Closed
Description: Cilantro On The Lake, located at Emerald Lake in Field, BC, offers a charming dining experience with picturesque views. Situated in a cozy cottage-style setting next to the lake, this restaurant provides guests with a warm and welcoming atmosphere to enjoy a meal. The menu features a variety of dishes prepared with care and attention to detail. Guests can savor delectable options such as pizza, soup of the day, lamb shanks, and more. The restaurant also offers takeaway service for those looking to enjoy their meal elsewhere. With friendly service and a comfortable ambiance, Cilantro On The Lake is an ideal spot for a relaxing dining experience amidst the beauty of nature.

The Siding Café
Location: 318 Stephen Ave, Field, BC V0A 1G0, Canada
Contact: +1 (250) 343-6380, **Website:** www.thesidingcafe.ca
Description: The Siding Café, nestled in the charming town of Field, British Columbia, offers a friendly and laid-back atmosphere, perfect for indulging in hearty comfort food. While temporarily closed, this café typically serves a diverse menu featuring breakfast, baked goods, and a variety of coffee options.

This cozy establishment is known for its welcoming ambiance and attentive service. Patrons can enjoy a selection of comfort grub, including veggie burgers, soups, and curry dishes. The café also boasts a surprisingly great collection of local beer and wine, making it an ideal spot to unwind and savor a delicious meal.

Despite its remote location, The Siding Café manages to deliver wonderful food, with standout items like their excellent fries receiving high praise from visitors. Whether you're stopping by for a quick bite during a long drive or seeking a satisfying meal after a day of exploring the surrounding area, The Siding Café offers a delightful dining experience in the heart of Field, British Columbia.

Velvet Antler Pottery

Location: 314 Stephen Ave, Field, BC V0A 1G0, Canada
Contact Information: +1 250-343-6456 | **Website:** velvetantlerpottery.com
Opening Hours: Monday - Sunday: 11 AM – 6 PM
Description: Velvet Antler Pottery, located in the picturesque town of Field, British Columbia, is a distinguished pottery store known for its exquisite, handcrafted ceramics. This family-run business captivates visitors with its range of unique pottery pieces, from decorative mugs to intricate art pieces, each showcasing the exceptional skill and creativity of the local artisans.

The shop offers a warm, welcoming atmosphere where visitors can explore an array of beautifully crafted items. The artisans at Velvet Antler Pottery are passionate about their craft, often sharing insights into their artistic process with customers. The store has become a favorite stop for those seeking original, high-quality handmade gifts that reflect the artistic heritage of the area.

ITINERARY

Whether you have just a single day to explore or a whole week to immerse yourself in the natural beauty and vibrant culture of the Canadian Rockies, our itineraries are structured to ensure you make the most of every moment. Each itinerary is crafted with practical timelines, must-see destinations, and insider tips to enhance your journey.

Day Trips

Banff in a Day

Exploring Banff National Park in a single day may seem ambitious given its vastness and the abundance of attractions, but with careful planning, you can enjoy a fulfilling experience that captures the essence of this magnificent park. Here's a recommended itinerary to make the most of your day in Banff.

Morning Activities:
1. **Sunrise at Lake Louise:**
    - **Experience:** Kick off your day with a sunrise viewing at Lake Louise. The early morning light casts a stunning glow on the turquoise waters, providing a peaceful and awe-inspiring start to the day.
    - **Activities:** After soaking in the sunrise, rent a canoe or kayak to gently paddle across the lake, surrounded by majestic mountain views.
2. **Hike to Lake Agnes Tea House:**
    - **Details:** This moderately challenging hike leads to the quaint Lake Agnes Tea House, nestled high in the mountains. It's a perfect spot to enjoy a warm beverage and light refreshments while admiring panoramic views of the surrounding wilderness.
    - **Duration:** Allow 2 to 3 hours for the hike and time at the tea house.

Afternoon Itinerary:
3. **Visit Moraine Lake:**
    - **Scenery:** Head over to Moraine Lake, located in the stunning Valley of the Ten Peaks. The lake's intense blue color and the dramatic peaks provide one of Canada's most photographed landscapes.
    - **Activity:** Explore the area via the Rockpile Trail, which offers one of the best views from the Rockpile Viewpoint.
4. **Drive the Bow Valley Parkway:**
    - **Travel:** As you return to Banff, drive along the scenic Bow Valley Parkway. This route is celebrated for its chances to spot wildlife and its breathtaking natural scenes.

Evening Activities:
5. **Banff Gondola Ride:**
   o **Experience:** Take the Banff Gondola up Sulphur Mountain for a spectacular aerial view of Banff and its surrounding peaks. The gondola ride is a must-do for first-time visitors seeking a unique perspective of the area.
   o **Sunset Views:** If timing allows, stay up at the summit to catch a stunning sunset.
6. **Dinner with a View:**
   o **Dining:** Enjoy a sumptuous dinner at Sky Bistro, located at the top of Sulphur Mountain. The restaurant offers a fine dining experience with panoramic views of the Canadian Rockies.

Nighttime Activities:
7. **Stroll Along Banff Avenue:**
   o **Leisure:** End your day with a leisurely stroll down Banff Avenue. Explore local shops, enjoy the vibrant street life, and perhaps finish the evening with live music or a show at one of the local pubs.

Optional Activities (If Time Allows):
- **Johnston Canyon Hike:** If your schedule permits, earlier in the day or the previous day, consider hiking through Johnston Canyon. It's renowned for its accessible walking paths that lead to stunning waterfalls and limestone canyons.
- **Banff Hot Springs:** For a relaxing end to your busy day, visit the Banff Upper Hot Springs and soak in the rejuvenating natural mineral waters.

Lake Louise Day Trip
Morning Activities:
- **Arrival and Sunrise:** Start your day early by arriving at Lake Louise to catch the breathtaking sunrise. The calm waters reflecting the golden light create a surreal experience that is both inspiring and peaceful.
- **Lakeshore Stroll:** After the sunrise, enjoy a relaxing walk around the lake. This easy path offers stunning views of the surrounding mountains and the grand Fairmont Chateau Lake Louise.
- **Canoeing/Kayaking:** Rent a canoe or kayak to explore the vibrant turquoise waters of Lake Louise. Paddling through this picturesque setting provides a unique perspective of the towering peaks and dense forests.

Afternoon Exploration:
- **Hike to Lake Agnes Tea House:** Begin a moderately challenging hike to the Lake Agnes Tea House. The trail meanders through lush forests and past cascading waterfalls, leading you to a quaint tea house nestled above Lake Agnes. Enjoy a refreshing cup of tea and snacks while soaking in the panoramic views.
- **Explore Mirror Lake and Big Beehive:** For those seeking a bit more adventure, continue from Lake Agnes up to Mirror Lake. From there, ascend to the Big Beehive for breathtaking vistas of Lake Louise and its alpine surroundings.

Optional Afternoon Activities:
- **Plain of Six Glaciers Tea House Hike:** If you're up for a longer challenge, the Plain of Six Glaciers Tea House hike offers an extended trail through spectacular landscapes, ending at another charming tea house with views of dramatic glaciers.
- **Horseback Riding:** Experience the beauty of Lake Louise on horseback, exploring trails that offer a unique vantage point of the lake and its environs.

Evening Wind Down:
- **Dinner with a View:** Return to the Fairmont Chateau Lake Louise for a sumptuous dinner at one of its acclaimed restaurants. Many dining options offer stunning views of the lake, providing a perfect backdrop to reflect on the day's adventures.
- **Stargazing:** Cap off your day by stepping outside to admire the star-filled sky. Lake Louise's minimal light pollution offers excellent conditions for stargazing, adding a magical finish to your visit.

Yoho Day Trip
Morning Activities:
- **Emerald Lake:** Start your day early at Emerald Lake, one of Yoho's most enchanting locations. Enjoy a peaceful stroll along the 5.2 km lakeshore trail, paddle across the serene turquoise waters by canoe, or simply relax and immerse yourself in the natural beauty around you.
- **Natural Bridge:** Next, visit the Natural Bridge, a remarkable rock formation carved by the force of the Kicking Horse River. This site offers a unique opportunity to see natural erosive forces at work, creating a stunning visual spectacle as the river flows through the carved stone.

Afternoon Exploration:
- **Takakkaw Falls:** Drive into the heart of Yoho Valley to witness Takakkaw Falls, one of the tallest waterfalls in Canada. The falls are a short walk from the parking area, offering easy access to incredible views. For those looking for a little more adventure, consider hiking the surrounding trails for different perspectives of the falls.
- **Spiral Tunnels Viewpoint:** Make a stop at the Spiral Tunnels Viewpoint to witness an engineering marvel of the Canadian Pacific Railway. Watch trains as they navigate the complex system of tunnels and tracks laid out through the steep terrain, a testament to human ingenuity and determination.

Evening in Field:
- **Village of Field:** Conclude your day with a visit to the quaint village of Field, the only town within Yoho National Park. Take a leisurely walk through the streets, explore local shops, and enjoy a hearty meal. Dining at Truffle Pigs Bistro is highly recommended for its delightful dishes and cozy atmosphere.

Optional Activities (If Time Allows):
- **Wapta Falls:** If you have extra time, hike to Wapta Falls, known for its impressive breadth and powerful flow. The hike is relatively easy and offers a rewarding view of the waterfall amid a picturesque setting.
- **Lake O'Hara:** For those who have managed to secure a reservation, a visit to the secluded Lake O'Hara area is a must. Known for its stunning alpine scenery and a network of rewarding trails, Lake O'Hara offers a more secluded and intensive hiking experience.

Multi-Day Itineraries
Day 1: Exploring Banff Town and Surroundings
Morning:
- **Breakfast at Wild Flour Bakery:** Start your day with a hearty breakfast at the Wild Flour Bakery on Bear Street, known for its artisanal breads and pastries—a local favorite.

Mid-Morning/Afternoon:
- **Banff Gondola Ride:** Take the Banff Gondola to the top of Sulphur Mountain. Enjoy breathtaking panoramic views of Banff, the Bow Valley, and the surrounding peaks. If you're up for it, explore the hiking trails at the summit or simply soak in the spectacular scenery.

Late Afternoon:
- **Scenic Drive on Bow Valley Parkway:** Take a leisurely drive along the Bow Valley Parkway. This scenic route offers beautiful views of the mountains and the Bow River, and keep an eye out for wildlife sightings.

Evening:
- **Dinner in Banff:** Enjoy dinner at one of Banff's renowned restaurants. Park Distillery Restaurant & Bar offers excellent locally crafted spirits and hearty dishes, or you might opt for Block Kitchen + Bar for inventive Canadian cuisine.

Day 2: Lake Louise and Moraine Lake
Morning:
- **Lake Louise:** Arrive early to avoid the crowds at Lake Louise. Enjoy a peaceful walk around the lake, taking in the stunning views of the turquoise waters against the backdrop of Victoria Glacier. For a more active morning, hike up to the Lake Agnes Tea House for spectacular views and a warm cup of tea.

Afternoon:
- **Moraine Lake:** Drive to Moraine Lake, a short distance from Lake Louise. Hike the Rockpile Trail, known for its exceptional views of the lake and the Valley of the Ten Peaks. This short but steep hike is well worth the effort for the breathtaking scenery.

Evening:
- **Return to Banff for Dinner:** Head back to Banff for the evening. For a casual meal, Eddie Burger Bar offers delicious burgers. For a more refined dining experience, consider The Maple Leaf, known for its excellent steaks and Canadian fare.

Optional Day 3: Emerald Lake and Natural Bridge in Yoho National Park

Morning:
- **Emerald Lake:** Drive west to Yoho National Park and visit Emerald Lake. Explore the lake by renting a canoe, hiking around its shores, or simply relaxing and enjoying the vibrant color of the waters.

Afternoon:
- **Natural Bridge:** Visit the Natural Bridge, an impressive natural rock formation sculpted by the Kicking Horse River. This quick stop is easily accessible from the parking area and offers a unique geological sight.
- **Late Afternoon/Evening:** If time permits, consider hiking to Takakkaw Falls, one of the tallest waterfalls in Canada, to marvel at its grandeur. Alternatively, return to Banff for a relaxing dinner to conclude your adventurous weekend.

One Week in the Rockies
Day 1-3: Banff National Park Exploration
Day 1: Arrival and Banff Introduction
- **Morning:** Arrive at Calgary International Airport, pick up your rental car, and drive to Banff. Check into your accommodation.
- **Afternoon:** Explore Banff Avenue, visiting shops, restaurants, and art galleries. Stop by the Whyte Museum of the Canadian Rockies to immerse yourself in the area's history and culture.
- **Evening:** Dine at Park Distillery Restaurant & Bar for local spirits and hearty dishes, or Block Kitchen + Bar for innovative Canadian cuisine.

Day 2: Iconic Landscapes and Relaxation
- **Morning:** Take the Banff Gondola up Sulphur Mountain for sweeping views. Optionally hike the Sulphur Mountain Boardwalk.
- **Afternoon:** Visit Lake Minnewanka, engage in activities like boating or lakeshore hiking.
- **Evening:** Unwind at the Banff Upper Hot Springs, enjoying the therapeutic mineral-rich waters.

Day 3: Active Exploration
- **Morning:** Hike the Tunnel Mountain Trail, offering excellent views over Banff.
- **Afternoon:** Drive along the scenic Bow Valley Parkway to Johnston Canyon and hike to the Lower and Upper Falls.
- **Evening:** Enjoy a final dinner in Banff before transitioning to Jasper.

Day 4-5: Jasper National Park Adventure
Day 4: Journey to Jasper
- **Morning:** Drive to Jasper via the Icefields Parkway, stopping at key spots like Bow Lake, Peyto Lake, and the Columbia Icefield.
- **Afternoon:** Arrive in Jasper, check into your accommodation, explore the town.
- **Evening:** Dine at a local restaurant in Jasper.

Day 5: Discovering Jasper's Gems
- **Morning:** Take a cruise on Maligne Lake to the iconic Spirit Island.
- **Afternoon:** Explore Maligne Canyon, hiking to view its waterfalls and geological formations.
- **Evening:** Ascend via the Jasper SkyTram to Whistlers Mountain for panoramic views.

Day 6: Kananaskis Country Outdoors
- **Morning:** Travel to Kananaskis Country, renowned for its vast outdoor activities.
- **Afternoon:** Choose from hiking to Grassi Lakes, mountain biking, or golfing in this picturesque region.
- **Evening:** Dine in Kananaskis Village or return to Canmore for additional dining options.

Day 7: Leisure in Canmore
- **Morning:** Spend the day in Canmore exploring art galleries, boutiques, and local shops.
- **Afternoon:** Visit the Canmore Museum and Geoscience Centre to explore the geological and historical aspects of the area.
- **Evening:** Conclude your trip with a memorable dinner in Canmore, celebrating a week of adventures and scenic delights.

GENERAL INFORMATION

Getting There and Around
Transportation options and tips for navigating within Banff, Lake Louise, Jasper, and Yoho.

By Air
Closest Major Airport: Calgary International Airport (YYC) is the gateway to the Rockies.
Transfers: From Calgary, you can rent a car, take a shuttle bus, or book a private transfer to reach Banff, Lake Louise, or Jasper.
By Train: VIA Rail offers picturesque train journeys to Jasper, with stops in major locations like Banff and Lake Louise. This option is perfect for those who prefer to relax and take in the scenery without the stress of driving.
By Car: The Trans-Canada Highway (Highway 1) provides direct access to Banff and Lake Louise, while the Icefields Parkway (Highway 93) is the scenic route connecting Lake Louise to Jasper.

Getting Around
Car Rental: Renting a car offers the most flexibility for exploring the Canadian Rockies, allowing access to more remote sites and the freedom to travel at your own pace.
Shuttle Buses: Shuttle services between Banff, Lake Louise, and Jasper are an excellent choice for those without a car. They provide a hassle-free way to move between parks and major attractions.
Public Transit: Local bus services operate in Banff and Canmore. Roam Transit offers routes around Banff and to some nearby attractions.
Taxis and Rideshares: Available in larger towns like Banff and Jasper, though they can be pricey, especially for longer distances.
Bike Rentals: Many areas within the parks are bike-friendly, with rental shops offering a range of bicycles for different terrains.
Hiking and Walking: The parks are filled with trails ranging from easy walks to challenging hikes, making foot travel a great option for nearby explorations.

Practical Tips
Advance Bookings: Both accommodations and transport should be booked well in advance, especially during the peak tourist seasons from June to August.
Park Pass: A valid park pass is required for entry into Banff and Jasper National Parks. Purchase online or at park gates.
Road Conditions: Always check current road conditions, particularly in winter, and drive carefully. Mountain roads can be tricky and unpredictable.
Fuel Up: Due to sparse gas stations in more remote areas, it's wise to fill up whenever possible.
Wildlife Safety: Maintain a safe distance from wildlife and follow all park guidelines to avoid disturbing the natural habitat.
Weather Preparedness: Mountain weather is notoriously changeable. Pack for all conditions: layers for cold, rainproof gear for showers, and sun protection.
Leave No Trace: Help preserve the parks' pristine nature by following Leave No Trace principles, including packing out all your trash.

Specific Area Tips
Banff: Utilize Roam Transit to avoid the hassle of parking, especially when visiting popular spots like Johnston Canyon.
Lake Louise: Parking fills quickly during summer. Arriving early or using a shuttle from Banff can save time and stress.
Jasper: Jasper's attractions are generally closer together, making it easier to explore on foot or by bike.
Yoho: Some roads, like the one to Takakkaw Falls, are unpaved and seasonally closed. Always verify road access and closures before setting out.

Weather Considerations for the Canadian Rockies
Traveling through the Canadian Rockies, you'll encounter a range of climates due to the vast changes in altitude and geography. Here's what to expect seasonally and how to best prepare for your visit:

Summer (June-August)
Temperatures: Expect warm days with temperatures ranging from 15°C to 25°C (59°F to 77°F). Nights can cool down to 5°C to 10°C (41°F to 50°F).

Weather Conditions: Mostly sunny days, though afternoon thunderstorms are common.

What to Wear: Lightweight, breathable layers are essential, along with a waterproof jacket for sudden downpours. Don't forget a sun hat, sunglasses, and sunscreen.

Autumn (September-October)

Temperatures: Days are cooler, ranging from 5°C to 15°C (41°F to 59°F), with chilly nights that can drop to 0°C to 5°C (32°F to 41°F).

Weather Conditions: Clear, sunny days are interspersed with rain and early snowfalls, especially at higher elevations.

What to Wear: Warm layers are crucial, including thermal wear, a heavy jacket, gloves, and a hat. Waterproof gear is recommended as precipitation is variable.

Winter (November-April)

Temperatures: Daytime temperatures hover between -5°C and -15°C (23°F to 5°F), with nights getting much colder, dropping between -15°C and -25°C (5°F to -13°F).

Weather Conditions: Snow is prevalent, particularly at higher altitudes, contributing to stunning winter landscapes but also to icy roads and paths.

What to Wear: Dressing in heavy, insulated layers is vital. Include a thermal base layer, a fleece mid-layer, and a windproof, waterproof outer layer. Insulated boots, gloves, and a warm hat are must-haves.

Spring (May-June)

Temperatures: Similar to autumn, temperatures range from 5°C to 15°C (41°F to 59°F) during the day and can chill down to 0°C to 5°C (32°F to 41°F) at night.

Weather Conditions: The weather can be quite unpredictable with a mix of sunny days, rain, and lingering snow at higher elevations.

What to Wear: Layering remains key during spring. Waterproof and windproof clothing will protect against sudden weather changes.

Packing Essentials
Essential Gear for All Seasons
Backpack: A comfortable daypack for carrying essentials like water, snacks, extra layers, and a camera.
Water Bottle or Hydration Reservoir: Staying hydrated is crucial, especially during hikes.
Snacks: Pack energy bars, trail mix, or fruit for quick fuel.
First-Aid Kit: Include basic supplies like bandages, antiseptic wipes, pain relievers, and blister treatment.
Navigation Tools: A map, compass, or GPS device can be helpful, especially for hiking.
Headlamp or Flashlight: Useful for early morning or late evening hikes, or in case of emergencies.
Sun Protection: Sunscreen, sunglasses, and a hat are essential, even in winter when the sun reflects off the snow.
Insect Repellent: Mosquitoes and other biting insects can be prevalent in the summer.
Camera: Capture the stunning scenery and wildlife.
Binoculars: Enhance your wildlife viewing experience.
Cash and Credit Cards: Some smaller establishments may not accept credit cards.
Travel Insurance: A good idea for any trip, especially one involving outdoor activities.

Summer Packing Checklist (June-August)
Hiking Boots or Shoes: Choose comfortable, sturdy footwear with good ankle support.
Hiking Socks: Moisture-wicking socks help prevent blisters.
Lightweight Hiking Pants or Shorts: Quick-drying and breathable fabrics are ideal.
Short-Sleeved and Long-Sleeved Shirts: Choose moisture-wicking fabrics.
Fleece Jacket or Vest: Provides warmth for cooler mornings and evenings.
Rain Jacket or Poncho: Be prepared for unexpected showers.
Hat: Protects from the sun.
Sunglasses: Shield your eyes from the bright sun.
Swimsuit: For enjoying lakes or hot springs.
Camp Chair (optional): For relaxing at scenic spots.

Winter Packing Checklist (November-April)
Insulated Winter Jacket: Choose a waterproof and windproof jacket for warmth.
Snow Pants or Bibs: Essential for staying dry and warm in the snow.
Warm Hat and Gloves or Mittens: Opt for waterproof and insulated options.
Thermal Base Layers: Top and bottom base layers made of wool or synthetic materials provide warmth and moisture-wicking.
Fleece or Wool Mid-Layers: Add extra insulation under your jacket.
Neck Gaiter or Scarf: Protects your neck and face from the cold.
Waterproof Winter Boots: Choose boots with good traction for icy conditions.
Warm Socks: Wool or synthetic socks are best for keeping your feet warm.
Hand and Foot Warmers (optional): Provide extra warmth on very cold days.
Sunglasses: Glare from the snow can be intense.
Ice Cleats or Traction Devices (optional): Helpful for hiking on icy trails.

Additional Tips:
Pack Light: Avoid overpacking by choosing versatile clothing items that can be layered.
Rent Gear: If you're not sure if you'll need certain items, consider renting them in Banff or Jasper.
Bring a Daypack for Hikes: Carry essentials like water, snacks, and extra layers on hikes.
Check Trail Conditions: Before heading out, check trail conditions and closures online or at visitor centers.

Made in United States
Troutdale, OR
07/19/2024

21416267R00083